The
Cottage
in the
Bog

Paddy Cummins

REVIEWS

A story as gentle and heart-warming as soft sunshine on an Irish summer's morn.

A charming, delightful story following one family's joys and trials living on a smallholding in Ireland, in the 1950's.

The vivid and evocative prose conjures up a simplistic way of living that is now gone forever but, thankfully, is lovingly and accurately recorded here by the author. Through it all, the beautiful Irish brogue can be heard singing off the pages, and the warmth and generosity of these lovely people stayed with me long after I finished this book.

Jenny Lloyd. Author of 'Leap the Wild Water'

***

A truly heart-warming memoir

A truly heart-warming memoir vividly depicting country life in Ireland in the early 50s. The rich prose immersed me right into the midst of that warm family and community feel in the countryside. Loved every page. A highly recommended read.

Dr. I. C. Camilleri. Malta.

***

A delightful Story

What a lovely memoir of what it was like growing up in Ireland in the early 50s. Clearly shining through was a strong sense of family and doing what was right. Selfless acts of kindness and generosity was simply a way of country life with both family and community. All of this was vividly depicted with care. Paddy made sure he got it right. 'His' story comes through on these pages realistically and was penned with a great eye for rich detail. A most enjoyable read.

Reviewed in the United States by P.A.

***

A trip back to a less complicated time

This was a wonderful read. Really enjoyed it. A peek back into Ireland in the early 50s when people still used pony and traps, made their own butter, sharing and relying on each other.

Really loved this book about old Ireland, so true to life and brilliantly written.

Babs17. United Kingdom.

***

A lovely book

This is a great family story, a simple tale, very enjoyable. I highly recommend it.

Magda. G.B.

***

To

Mammy and Daddy

With Love

The
Cottage
in the
Bog

Paddy Cummins

MOVING

The big van shuddered to a halt in front of the red and white gates that blocked the roadway to traffic, and opened the railway to trains.

"Oh great," shouted Robbie, "a train; can we get out to see it?"

"Yeah, yeah, c'mon, c'mon" shouted Paschal, "c'mon Timmy, c'mon Kenny."

Mina was asleep on the mattress in the back.

"No, yis can't, stay where yis are," said their mother, half turning her head. "Yis'll see it well enough."

"Ah Mammy."

Robbie turned his pleading eyes to his father, who was resting his elbows on the steering wheel, easing the stress after driving the big unfamiliar van and his precious cargo twenty-five miles non-stop from the outskirts of Waterford City.

"Daddy, please, tell Mammy to let us out, we never saw a train so near; please Daddy."

"Yis'll see trains every day from now on, yis'll be sick of 'em."

"I won't be sick of 'em," said Timmy, "I love the big steam injin's, an' the smell of 'em."

Mina opened her eyes and sat up. "Are we there yet?"

"Not yet" said Robbie, "get up here quick an' see the big train flyin' by."

They wriggled their way through the assorted household items to get the best possible view.

The noise was deafening. The van swayed and vibrated as the steam engine and forty goods wagons thundered by. The long silence that followed was only broken by the clinking sound of locks being opened by the elderly gatekeeper. As the van rolled through, Markie Kehoe, recognising Tom at the wheel, smiled warmly and waved to the family.

Tom didn't bother to change into second gear. Hugging the left side of the road, he swung the van in a wide arc into the narrow lane that twisted its way to an isolated area known as The Bogside.

"Now for the bumps; hould tight," he said, smiling as he dodged the worst hazards and the van zigzagged along.

He knew every deep pothole and high stone from years of walking and biking it, but manoeuvring the big wide vehicle through such rough and narrow terrain was a new experience. He loved driving, and when his boss arranged the loan of the van for the day, he relished the challenge. He could do anything with tractors and knew he could manage the big van too.

Molly leaned forward and cleared the foggy windscreen with the back of her hand. It was still only mid-day, but it looked like dusk. The wet, winter landscape spread out at each side of the waterlogged lane. Bare hedges, leafless shrubs, ditches overflowing into the low-lying fields, the sky, a low grey canopy of gloom enveloping the dark and dreary landscape. She knew it was only January and it wouldn't always be like that, but the dark, forlorn scene that confronted her, didn't ease the apprehensions she silently harboured about this move. The rocky lane, long and lonely, got even worse as it wound its way parallel with the railway line into the wilderness of the bog. In bygone days several families inhabited the old isolated bog side, but now only two dwellings remained: the little thatched homestead where Tom was born and reared, and further on, Johnny and Lizzie Moran's small farm.

The children were on their knees looking sharply over the shoulders of their father and mother.

"We're goin' very slow," said Robbie, "we'll never get there."

"I don't want to break a spring," his father replied.

Molly twisted sideways, turning to face the children.

"Now, whatever Granny says to any of yis; don't be cheeky and answer 'er back. D'yis all hear me now. Yis know she is very old and sick and we have to get used to 'er."

They answered with nods of acceptance. It was something she was drilling into them for the previous week.

She turned to Tom. He kept his eyes on the lane.

"I don't know what's goin' to happen, Tom, I'm not sure at all." Her voice was low and just reached his ear.

"Ah, t'will be alright, she'll be glad to see us; she's gone very shook."
He kept his voice down too.

"Yeah, but ye know what she's like."

"Ah, she's gone down a lot."

He swung the van around the sharp bend that took them away from
the railway line, into the final stretch of uneven laneway, and the white-
washed gable of the little thatched house came into view. Timmy leaned
forward between his parent's shoulders, pointing towards the house.

"Robbie look, d'ye see that winda?"

All eyes focused on the little window high up in the apex of the
gable.

"Aint that great, Robbie, we can go up there an' see all the trains
goin' by."

Tom stopped the van, leaned on the steering wheel and surveyed the
old familiar entrance to his beloved homestead. The old wooden gate was
sagging and barely standing between the ivy-clad stone piers. The short
lane that led up to the house was grass-covered, except for a narrow path
in the middle. The overgrown hedges were a transparent brown, and the
big beach tree was naked and desolate. Molly moved to get out.

"No, stay where ye are, I'll open it." He stepped down on to the
soggy grass, stretched his arms and carefully lifted the gate open. He
measured with his eyes the width of the van against the entrance, got
back in and reversed, allowing him to make a wide swing to negotiate
the narrow opening. He had to make two reversals before finally easing
through with only an inch to spare at each side.

The little yard, enclosed by a circle of assorted small outhouses was
also grassy, but had a series of paths criss-crossing in various directions.
The door of the old thatched cottage was shut and the two sash windows,
draped with faded lace curtains, looked unopened for years. When Tom
switched off the van engine, they all waited, looked around and filled
their anxious eyes. The silence was eerie, the atmosphere gloomy, and
Molly felt a nervous tension and a terror, akin to having received a life
sentence for a decision of folly, taken with the best of intentions.

The door slowly opened, but only a few inches. The big red van
filling the yard hadn't yet revealed its contents and precautions were being taken. Tom got out, the door gradually opened fully, framing the
slim figure of his mother. She looked frail and stooped, her slate-grey
hair combed back into a bun, staring through her thick glasses and clad

from head to toe in her widow black. She shuffled forward, looking slightly bewildered, but seemed to be relieved to have identified the source of the invasion.

"Ah, it's you Tom, that's an awful big yoke, how will you turn it?"

"Ah, I'll manage it; how are you?"

"I'm better now." She coughed her usual wheezy cough. "I was poorly with the flu."

Molly got out, followed by the children.

"The whole gang are here now," said Tom, "an' the van is full o' stuff."

"Ah, sure I know, ye can empty it later."

Molly shook the old lady's bony hand.

"How are you, Granny?"

"I'm better now … how are you? …you put on a lot of weight."

Molly didn't reply. The children lined up to shake their grandmother's hand. There were no hugs or kisses. They knew that Granny wasn't like that.

*

Molly was jaded but still couldn't relax. She kept moving around the little kitchen with the mug of tea in her hand.

"Will ye sit down before ye fall down," said Tom, as he sat at the end of the table, tucking into the sandwiches she had made for him. It was almost midnight and the house was now quiet after many hours of hustle and bustle, trying to fit the family into the little shack that was really too small to accommodate them.

The children, exhausted after their long day, were now sound asleep upstairs in the inside room. Granny, who stayed most of the evening in her chair by the fireside, keeping a keen eye on the work without interfering, was now in bed. Her snug bedroom, accessed through the dainty little parlour, was strictly private and would not be disturbed. Tom and Molly would soon retire to the other little bedroom upstairs, just big enough for their double bed and a small bunk bed for Mina.

Molly sat down, still wondering if there was something else to be down.

"Are ye sure there's nothin' left in the van, Tom?"

"I'll make sure in the morn' before I go."

"What time will ye be goin'?"

"It'll take an hour. The van must be back at eight, I better go at seven."

"We'll have to be up at six so."

"That'll do."

"Y'ill be tired," Molly said, "go to bed early tomorrow night.."

"I will."

" Will ye be lonesome?"

"Ah no, sure I'll have to get used to it."

Y'ill surely miss the children.'

"Ah sure…."

"Even if ye won't miss me…?"

His wan smile and sad eyes gave her the answer she had expected.

"Y'ill be down on Saturday, what time will ye get here?"

"I'll have te work 'till one. T'will take me an hour to get to Passage on the bike. If I can get the ferry quick I'll be here between three and four."

"Y'ill make it before dark then?"

"Oh, I will,"

"I'll have to get some shoppin'," Molly opened the door of the press. "What's in there won't last long."

"Johnny Moran goes to Campile every Friday; he calls here on the way."

"Yeah," said Molly, "but I'd like to have me own way of goin'."

"Maybe we might get the ass an' car goin' again," said Tom, "we'll see at the weekend."

"I'll have te get somethin' anyway, ye couldn't be stuck here with nothin'."

Molly raised her hand to count on her fingers the things she had to do, and the places she had to go.

"I have to go to the school to get the children enrolled. We have to go to Mass on Sunday. I want to go see Nellie in Ballycullane and Nan in Aclare. And sure if I don't go te see Nicky in Haggard, I'll never live it down."

"Ah sure, y'ill get around to all that after a while."

"I know Tom, but I'll get nowhere without a way of goin'; I haven't even a bike."

"I know, I know, we'll see about the ass."

It wasn't an old crippled ass Molly was thinking about, something faster and better. Being near to her brother and sisters and visiting them was one little bonus that helped make up her mind to leave the comfort of Waterford, and come here to live and care for Tom's mother, a move she dreaded, and resisted for two years. She knew it was fraught with all kinds of trials and tribulations, things that Tom could never see because he was born and reared here. This was always his home, Granny was his mother, he was her son and he could handle her. Anyway, she was here now and she was ready for it. If it all went wrong she'd have to suffer it, but it wouldn't be her fault, she'd do her best.

*

Molly and her five children stood in the freezing darkness of the yard, waving goodbye to Tom as he eased the big van through the narrow gateway and swung left down the lane. They watched the lights grow dimmer as he slowly crept along by the railway, through the railway gates and away to Waterford. As she watched, Molly filled with mixed emotions. This was *it* now. Tom was gone. He'll be back every weekend, but from now on she will have to manage without him. She could feel the weight of the burden already. Tom wouldn't be there to rescue her if things went wrong. His patience, his calm and relaxed way of looking at things was the complete opposite to her. She wished she could be like that, but she had that from her mother, it was in her nature; she couldn't help it.

The children were shivering in the frosty fog of the dark early morning. "C'mon,' she said, we'll make a pot of porridge, that'll warm yis up."

The little turf fire had died down. Small blocks of wood, which they had brought from Waterford, were placed on it. Paschal sat on the three-legged stool, turning the fan wheel; soon the fire was red, the kettle singing, and the pot boiling. The children sat on long forms at both sides of the table filling up with hot porridge, smothered in milk and sweetened with plenty of sugar. They hadn't yet got used to the little cramped kitchen; such a change compared to the big spacious one they had in Waterford. They were almost touching as they moved around on the flagstone floor, but it was cute and cosy, with the heavy embossed wallpaper, the glowing red fire and the soft warm light of the paraffin wall lamp.

A rolling drone of sound and a shrill blast of a whistle sparked immediate panic reaction among the children. They rushed up the almost straight, ladder-like stairs that led to the little gable window. It was the morning passenger train from Rosslare Harbour to Limerick Junction, and would stop at all the stations along the way, including the big one, Waterford. Five little heads squeezed into the recess of the window and ten excited eyes filled with wonder. They watched as the big steam engine puffed and pulled a long line of brightly-lit carriages through their vision, before fading and disappearing over the brow of Knokea hill. Timmy was overwhelmed with excitement. He rushed down to breathlessly update his mother, who listened attentively, before clamping him in a big hug. The others soon returned to help tidy up, as their mother wanted to make sure that everything was in order for Granny's arrival.

*

Molly put her ear to the door of Granny's bedroom and hearing her cough and move around, concluded that she was up and would soon be arriving in the kitchen. She checked the weather, which was a big improvement on yesterday – dry but cold.

"Can we go see the ass, Mammy?" asked Paschal.

"Oh yeah," said Robbie excitedly, "can we ride him?"

"Yeah, me too, Mammy," Timmy made sure he wasn't going to be left out.

Kenny and Mina were upstairs taking their toys and things out of a cardboard box.

"Yeah, I suppose yis can," said Mammy, seeing the benefit of a less populated kitchen when Granny came up from her room.

"Now, Paschal," she warned, "you mind the others and don't let 'em go too near the ass; he might be afraid of yis and kick or bite."

"Ah, we'll talk nice to'im," said Paschal, "sure he's only a little ass, Mammy."

"Oh, yeah," said Timmy, "will we bring 'em somtin' t'eat?"

"Yeah," exclaimed Robbie, "a carrot."

"All right then, get one in the cupboard – only a small one now."

They skipped across the little haggard, through the small paddock and out to the two-acre grass field, which was the total area of the little holding. Having swept the field with anxious eyes, they failed to see the ass. The hedges were very overgrown - briars and bushes extended several yards out - and the boys decided to walk around to see if he was hiding somewhere.

Beyond the far corner of the field they could see Moran's house and farmyard. An assortment of loud animal voices could be heard.

"Why are they shoutin'?" asked Timmy.

"They're hungry," said Robbie.

"It's probably their breakfast time," said Paschal.

They walked around two sides of the square field without finding the ass. looking for an opening in the hedges for signs of his escape; there was none. On their way down the far side they found him lying relaxed in a little sheltered area between thick furze bushes. The three boys stood transfixed admiring the grey donkey with the dark cross on his back. Pointing his long ears forward, he seemed to be undecided whether to make a quick getaway or stay in his comfortable little nest. Paschal eased his way towards him holding out the carrot and told the others to stay back and block off the exit. Having smelt the carrot and rejected it, the ass jumped to his feet. Paschal patted him gently on the neck and along his back. He seemed to enjoy that and soon he was surrounded by his new friends and being showered with love and affection.

*

The creaking of footsteps on the floorboards of the parlour signalled the arrival of Granny. When she entered the kitchen she paused to have a sweeping look around, before settling herself in her chair beside the blazing fire of hissing wood.

"How are ye to-day, Granny?" Molly was at the table mixing the ingredients for a cake of bread.

"I'm not too bad now. But the chest was bothering me all night, I can't get rid of it."

"It's probably the weather," said Molly, "I'll get yer breakfast in a minute."

"What's it doing outside?"

"It's dry and after brightenin' up a bit; but it was very cold and frosty when Tom was headin' off this mornin'."

"I heard the Van. Where's the children?"

Paschal, Robbie and Timmy are over in the field with the ass and Kenny and Mina are upstairs playing with toys.'

"Oh yes, the poor donkey, he's getting very old, like myself."

"Tom was sayin' he might yoke him at the weekend."

"Oh no he can't. Sure that poor animal is retired long ago, his yoking days are gone."

Molly didn't reply.

"When will you be going to shop?' Granny pointed to the press, 'it must be getting low in there."

"Tom said that Johnny Moran goes to Campile every Friday, I'll have to ask him for a lift."

"Yes, he have a motor car; he brings me the things every week."

"I'll go over to see him."

Molly hung the baking pot on the crane over the fire. It hadn't been used for years and had to be scrubbed clean. She waited a minute for it to warm, floured it, laid in the large cake and placed the cover on it. She then placed an egg in the saucepan beside the fire and wet a pot of tea from the big black kettle. Soon the tray of breakfast – tea, boiled egg and buttered bread – was on a chair in front of Granny.

"Is that alright now?" asked Molly.

Granny answered "yes" by nodding her head, while she struggled through a bout of wheezy coughing.

*

She buttoned the little coat up to Kenny's neck, turned up the collar and covered his ears with a knitted beret. Mina was well wrapped in her pink coat, scarf and woollen pixie cap. Molly checked her own appearance in the mirror in the hall, tucking the ends of her headscarf under the collar of her heavy brown coat. It would be her first visit to Moran's; she didn't know Johnny or his elderly mother, but according to Tom, they were nice people.

She wondered why the boys hadn't returned – they were now gone almost two hours – she would try to locate them on her way over to Moran's.

"Will you be okay now, Granny?" she asked, stoking the fire and tidying the hearth.

"I will, I will of course, she said, fingering her rosary beads, 'I'll be saying my prayers."

"I'll go then, and when I come back, I'll do your room."

"Yes, all right, thanks."

On her way through the yard, Molly and her two youngest children went on a circular tour of inspection. She was curious to see behind the old wooden doors of the little outhouses. They hadn't been opened for years but she managed to move the slide bolts and pull them open. A miniature cow house with two stalls and tying chains prompted thoughts of fresh milk and butter in abundance, if only it was inhabited. The henhouse smelt ghastly, but the roosts and nest boxes were still intact. The low stone building at the corner had a narrow entrance out into a little yard enclosed by a small iron gate. This, Molly saw, was the piggery and she could almost hear the grunts and squeals of little pigs. The shed, built with timber and galvanised sheeting had a door the full width of its gable. Inside, it had a division which provided a stable at the back, and a tool and car shed at the front. The old donkey's car rested on its shafts and the tackling, together with an assortment of old tools, were spread along a timber bench.

"Can we get cows an' hens an pigs?" asked Mina, "Oh please mammy, I'd love 'em."

"Oh yeah," said Kenny, "little chickens."

"Where would we get the money, Mina? We'd have to buy them, ye know."

"I'll give ye the money in me moneybox," said Mina.

"Ah, I know ye would, Pet," she said, clasping both of them to her sides.

"C'mon, we'll go over te see Johnny Moran an' his mother."

The lane to Moran's ran parallel with the two-acre field where Molly expected to find her three sons and the donkey. The hedgerow was high and dense and at the first low spot she climbed the bank, to be confronted with a scene that startled her. A large grey donkey, ridden by one boy and led by two boys was approaching briskly towards her. Paschal and Robbie walked at each side of the donkey's head leading him, while sitting proudly on board was Timmy, smiling broadly.

"Paschal," she shouted, "the child will fall off and get hurt."

The boys steered towards their mother.

"I'd never fall off, Mammy, I'm goin' to be a jockey when I grow up."

"He is, Mammy," said Robbie, "he's great an' he's not a bit afraid."

"C'mon now, we're goin' over to Moran's, let the ass go an' come with us."

"Ah, Mammy," said Paschal, "Robbie an' me didn't get a ride yet."

"Yeah," pleaded Robbie, "just two more times around the field, we'll be over after yis."

"Well, don't be long an' don't fall off an' hurt yourselves."

"We won't, Mammy," three relieved voices said in unison.

She held the hands of Mina and Kenny as she continued towards Moran's. She studied the landscape and noticed how the lane divided the land so starkly. To her left the bog spread out in a wet, level expanse that reached all the way to the railway line, while all the land on her right was dry, fertile, and climbed steadily to the distant horizon. Moran's farm seemed to straddle the lane, half of it bog and half dry land.

As she approached the wide entrance she could hear the sound of an engine and some loud hammering. The slated farmhouse looked out on the big square yard which was surrounded by sheds, and crowded with an assortment of vehicles, carts, machinery and scrap, abandoned haphazardly in no particular order. Through a sagging wooden gate leading to the haggard, she could see a rick of hay, two ponies, some cows and calves, hens and ducks and a big sow lying on her side, grunting happily as she suckled a big family of piglets.

The hammering and the engine sound was coming from a big shed with a wide entrance and the noise stopped abruptly as she crossed the yard towards the house.

"Hello, hello, hello," the friendly greeting came from the big shed.

"Hello," said Molly, she could see him emerging through a fog of dust, "you must be Johnny."

He was now approaching her, smiling broadly, exposing a full set of prominent teeth through a face powdered with sawdust. He was a tall, lean, well built, lively man, that she estimated to be around fifty.

"Christ God, I am, the very fella, I'm Johnny Moran."

"I'm Molly Coonan, Tom's wife, we're goin' to be your new neighbours."

"Well Christ God, I'm pleased to meet ye," he wiped his hands on his trouser legs before shaking her hand with gusto. "Y'er as welcome as the flowers in May, an' who have we here?"

"This is Mina and this is Kenny; say hello to Johnny."

Kenny greeted him clearly, but Mina, shy as usual, smiled and kept her gaze on the ground.

"Is that the whole family now?"

"Oh God no, I've three boys as well."

"Christ God, five, that's great, where are they?"

"They'll be over here soon, that's if they can leave the ass in the field, they'll have the poor oul fella killed ridin' him."

"Ah sure, chaps'll be chaps, I was the same meself. Christ God, c'mon in, c'mon in, me mother'll be delighted te meet yis."

Alerted by the sound of conversation in the yard, Lizzy Moran was on her way out to investigate. They met in the hallway, Johnny introduced his mother to Molly, the two women shook hands warmly and they all entered the warm, spacious kitchen. Molly had learned from Tom of Lizzy Moran's back problem that caused her to walk with her head and upper body bent down to the level of her waist. She was a slim, white-haired, active woman, and although in her early eighties, it didn't bother her at all.

"Sit down there now and I'll make the tea." She went to the corner cupboard, got two bars of chocolate, and gave them to Mina and Kenny.

"Oh begor, Mother always have the goodies," said Johnny, addressing the children, "an' she's great at hidin' 'em."

"Don't mind him, I wouldn't have much left if he knew where they were; he's still a big child."

The kettle was boiling on the red-hot turf fire, Johnny took down the decorative tea box from the mantelpiece, spooned it in, and poured a full pot. As Lizzy was setting the table, Molly gave her the ages of all her children.

"Aren't you great; you have your hands full and now you're going to look after all them and care for Tom's mother as well."

"I know, said Molly, I must be a glutton for punishment."

"Christ God, send the chaps over te me an' I'll keep em happy, said Johnny, I'll make men out of 'em."

"Don't be silly, Johnny,' said his mother, ye know they have to go to school – don't mind him, Molly, that fella says quare things."

Molly enjoyed the tea, especially the lovely hot scones and strawberry jam and thanked Lizzy.

"I love baking, but with only the two of us here, we don't need much. I'll be able to do more baking now for my new neighbours."

Molly was really impressed with the friendliness, warmth and generosity.

"How will ye manage for the shopping, asked Lizzy, will ye need a lift?"

"I'm afraid so," said Molly, Tom was goin' to yoke the ass an' car but Granny says the ass is too old."

"Christ God, said Johnny, I have the very thing for ye, a grand little pony."

"But what would she put behind him," his mother asked, "she'd need a trap."

"Sure I have one o' them too."

"The one with the broken shaft?"

"Aye, sure I'd be no length puttin' a shaft in it – half a day is all t'would take me."

"Hold on," said Molly, "that's all great but would I be able to afford it?"

"Afford it! Christ God sure the oul pony is wasted out there in the haggard, an' the trap is only in me way out there in the workshop."

"Now Molly," said Lizzy, "'tis **you** that's doin' **him** a favour."

"Oh Johnny, I don't know how to thank ye enough; that would be a God-send."

"Say no more, I'll have ye fixed in a couple of days, an' ye can go wherever ye like then."

"I'll never stop praying for ye, thanks Johnny,"

"A few prayers wouldn't go astray on him," said his smiling mother.

Johnny spotted the boys in the yard.

"Christ God, the chaps are here," he rushed out.

"Morra me hardy fellas…wha' way a yis?"

"Well, thanks," said Paschal.

"What'll I call yis, lads?"

"I'm Paschal."

"Oh, begor, a great name. An' yersef?"

"I'm Robbie."

"Powerful, after Robert Emmett, begor."

"An' this little man here?"

"Timmy"

"Good man Timmy. Christ God, them are great names…Paschal, Robbie and Timmy… Paschal, Robbie, Timmy…Now I have yis."

"What's your name?" asked Timmy.'

"Christ God, they calls me everything, but me rale name is Johnny."

"C'mon in, lads, I bet yis'd drink tay."

"We would," said Timmy.

Molly was impressed by Johnny's faultless introduction of her three boys to his mother.

"Hey, Mother, will ye listen to these great names."

The boys looked uncomfortable standing in front of the old woman bent down to their height. Laying his big rough hand on each of their heads he called out: "This is Paschal, this is Robbie and this is, me brave Timmy."

His mother shook hands with them and gave them a bar of chocolate each from the corner cupboard. After finishing their tea, scones and jam, Johnny leaned in over them at the table.

"A' yis full now, lads?"

"We are, thanks," they replied together.

"C'mon so, I want te show yis."

He led them to an adjoining room, beckoning the younger ones to come too.

"We'll be back in a few minutes."

His mother smiled and turned to Molly.

"That's his music room, you'll hear him now in a minute."

"He's great with children" said Molly.

"He'd spend the whole day with them."

Rousing music and song erupted from the room.

"Oh, that's wonderful, isn't he great?"

"He's putting on a concert for them now. He's worse than any child himself."

Lizzy sat near Molly for a little quiet chat.

"How is herself?"

"She's very chesty and weak."

"Ah yes, that old bronchitis, she's had it for years and this old weather doesn't help – God, you'll have your hands full caring for her."

"I know," said Molly, "and sometimes she's not the easiest to manage."

"Ah sure, the poor creature is very set in her ways. She was unfortunate – no sooner had the family grown up and gone, when poor Mike died and left her all those years on her own."

"Tom thinks she's gone down a lot – he sees a big change in her this winter – that's why we had to come."

"And did she mind the children coming?"

"Oh, I suppose she wasn't all that happy, but Tom told her it was either that, or go to the County Home – she'd die before she'd go there."

"What about the rest of the family, do they come to see her?"

Peader has a big job in Waterford and Tim is workin' the little farm outside Campile that he got from his aunt. They come an odd time, but the two nuns are in Rome; so they couldn't come.'

"She's very lucky to have Tom and yourself – what would she do without yis?"

"Ah sure," said Molly, "we try to do our best, but you'd wonder if she appreciates it at all."

"Oh, I'd say she do, but she's the kind that wouldn't show it."

The room door opened.

"Mammy, Mammy, c'mere 'till ye see this." Timmy was all excited.

She followed him into the room, stopped, and wide-eyed, marvelled at the scene and the sound that confronted her. Musical instruments were strewn everywhere: On one sofa was a fiddle, a melodeon and a guitar, and on another lay a set of bagpipes and piano accordion. Johnny was belting out a lively tune on a big upright piano and singing at the same time. Robbie was all legs and arms banging away behind a set of drums in the corner, and in the other corner, Paschal, the bohran player, was moving, swaying and trying his best to keep up with the rhythm. Johnny indicated the end by rising to a crescendo, and when silence returned he stood up and clapped the boys.

"Christ God, they're great musicians – we'll have a band in no time."

Molly laughed and they all returned to the kitchen. Lizzy handed Molly a can of milk and a biscuit-tin full of scones.

"I don't know how to thank ye," said Molly, feeling emotional from all the kindness.

"I'll have that transport fixed up for ye t'morrow," said Johnny, "I'll be over when I have it all ready."

"Oh, God bless ye, Johnny, but how will I pay ye?"

"Put that out of yer head now, me good woman, an' have a bit a sense."

Lizzy saw them out. They waved and smiled their way through the yard and on to the lane.

*

The forenoon on Thursday had brought pleasure and excitement to Molly and the children. It was all thanks to Johnny Moran who drove into the yard in the pony and trap at ten o'clock and exclaimed: "Now Missis, ye can travel the country at yer heart's content."

The children surrounded him, dancing with delight; Molly was close to tears, felt like giving him a big bear hug, but managed to restrain herself. The trap, mahogany with black wheels, was the perfect fit for the little black pony. It was freshly varnished, had red cushions on the seats, a door with a brass handle, and an iron step behind. The pony seemed to have had a make-over too – brushed hair, mane and tail cut, new shoes, and the harness clean and supple from a dressing of leather oil.

"Oh, Johnny, I never expected anything as good as this; ye shouldn't have gone to all that trouble."

"Ah, will ye whisht woman; ye couldn't call that trouble – a labour of love, I'd call it."

"What's his name?" shouted Timmy.

"His name?" Christ God, he have no name a tall, a tall; yis can think of a name for 'em yerselves.'

"We sure will," said Timmy.

"Now, we'll go for a little spin," said Johnny, "but we won't all fit in."

"I'll go first, with you and Mina and Kenny," said Molly, "and then we'll bring the boys."

Johnny gave Molly the reins and a few tips on driving, and without a problem, she drove down to the railway gates and back again.

Johnny got out. "Christ God, yer an expert now, I'll let yis work away."

He watched and waited while Molly drove all the children to the railway gates, and when they returned he showed them how to yoke and unyoke the pony.

"Now," he said, "yis can let 'em out with the ass; they'll be grand together."

"Can we ride em?" asked Robbie.

"Christ God, course ye can…he's as quiet as a mouse."

He left them with a chorus of "Thanks Johnny" following him.

When they released the pony in the haggard, he galloped through the little paddock and out into the field, where he met up with the donkey and they both circled the field in a getting-to-know-you canter. Molly decided that the trap shouldn't be left out in the yard under the weather and, helped by the boys, tried to fit it into the shed beside the old donkey's car. There wasn't enough room for both so the car was pulled out, the trap rolled in, and the harness placed neatly on the bench. When the door of the shed was closed and the old car put tidily against the wall, the happy family moved into the house for some lunch and to update Granny on the morning's activities.

*

The pale afternoon sun cast a rare beam through the kitchen window, prompting Granny to rise from her fireside chair and to shuffle outside for her little daily stroll. She went only as far as the gate at the end of the short lane, took a long sweeping look over the bog and came slowly back again. On her return she spotted the donkey's car by the wall. She stopped, and in a hoarse, agitated voice, called Molly.

"What's the car doing there?"

"Oh," said Molly, "it wouldn't fit in the shed with the trap."

"But it always fitted in the shed."

Molly, stunned and mystified, had to think fast.

"We'll put it back in."

The old lady didn't reply but shuffled back into the house. Molly and the children took out the trap, and put the car back in the shed. Concealing the humiliation and distress that filled her, she tried to explain to the children that Granny was old-fashioned, set in her ways, and because she was the owner of everything, she had to be obeyed.

*

His sides heaving, his nostrils blowing and his neck sweating, the little pony relished the respite when he was tied to the ring in the wall outside the school. He had taken Molly and the five children the two-mile journey that climbed steadily most of the way and steeply up the final hill to the little stone building at the turn of the road. It was Friday and Molly wanted to get Paschal, Robbie and Timmy enrolled, so that they could start school on Monday morning.

Miss Harty, the Principal, and the only teacher, greeted them warmly, enrolled the boys and introduced them to the sixty other children, boys and girls of various ages, seated behind ancient desks, schoolbags beside them on the old wooden floor. It was one long room with tall windows at each side and a large fireplace at the top end where the teacher's desk and the blackboards were also placed.

The teacher showed the boys the desks they would occupy and said the toilet was outside behind the school and the playground was the road. She explained to Molly how the seven different classes were organised. Infants were in the first desk at the front, and sixth class was in the desk at the back. In between, the classes were like steps of stairs. Having seen the modern facilities at the big school in Waterford, Molly asked Miss Harty how it could be possible for one teacher to manage and educate seven classes of children, ranging in ages from six to thirteen.

"Oh, it's really not a problem; we manage fine. In my thirty years here, past pupils of this little school have become priests, nuns, doctors, teachers, engineers and many of them are scattered all over the world."

"Well congratulations," said Molly, "I hope these boys will work hard and become somethin' too."

"Of course they will; I'll see you boys, please God, on Monday."

*

"Ye can tie em here Missis, I'm headin' home now."

"Oh, thanks," said Molly, as the little man backed the white cob and a cart full of shopping out from the wall of horses, ponies and donkeys. She got the pony in and tied him to the ring. It was her first shopping day in the little village and was all new to her.

"Is it always this busy?"

"No Mam …only on a Saturday …any other day an yis'd have any 'mount o' room. God be with yis now."

"God be with you too, an' thanks,"

He hopped up on the side lace of the cart and with his legs dangling, shook the reins at the cob. "Gwan Boy" he ordered, and as he headed up the road, Molly, Mina and Kenny crossed the concrete yard and entered the Co-Op Store.

The big shop was crowded, full of chatter and activity. Shelves, packed with goods, lined the walls from floor to ceiling, the grocery counter ran the full length, at one end was the meat counter and at the other was the hardware department. Brown-coated assistants were working as fast as they could, but seemed to be under pressure trying to cope with the throngs of customers waiting to be served.

The hive of activity was heightened by the noisy overhead cable system that criss-crossed the shop, bringing each customer's invoice and payment in a wooden canister to the cash office and returning at speed with the stamped receipt and the change. Mina and Kenny were fascinated watching the little boxes flying in all directions over their heads.

"What makes 'em go?" asked Mina.

Mammy looked up. "They work on springs …when the man pulls the little rope, the spring makes it go."

"Will our money go in it?" asked Kenny.

"T'will," said his mother, "an, then we'll have no money left."

"Ah, but Mammy, we'll have the shoppin'," said Mina.

"You're a clever girl, Mina."

Most shoppers, including Molly, had long written lists that the shop assistants had to transfer in handwriting to their invoice books. Then each item had to be got – some weighed and wrapped – and packed neatly in shopping bags. The bill had to be totted up, payment received, invoice and money dispatched to the cash office, and the invoice and customer's change checked on its return.

Molly and the children carried the bags to the trap but she wasn't finished yet. She had a docket for flour, wheaten meal and paraffin oil, which had to be weighed and measured by the man in the outside store, and she had to cross the road to the chemist shop for Granny's medication.

After two hours, it was time to untie the pony and head for home.

"I'm hungry," said Kenny.

"Me too," said Mina.

"'Tis the biscuits in the bag that's makin' yis hungry," said their smiling Mammy. After some rummaging in the shopping bags, the goodies emerged and the three of them chewed their way down the village, out past the police barracks, and on towards Sutton's Hill.

*

Paschal and Robbie were out in the yard playing a match with an old punctured football. The goalposts were two big stones, and they took turns at being goalkeeper and outfield player. Timmy was inside, nestled high in the little gable window, his eyes longingly focussed down the lane to the railway gates, hoping to see his mother, sister and brother approaching in the pony and trap with the week's shopping, including some sweet goodies, and maybe even a few surprises.

Granny was in her fireside chair fingering her beads and the house was silent except for her bouts of laboured coughing and the ticking of the clock on the mantelpiece. The boys were keeping out of her way after she had chastised them, and made them release the donkey back into the field. They were looking forward to an enjoyable morning while their mother was in Campile, but it all turned sour when Granny heard them laughing and chattering in the yard, as they prepared the donkey for a couple of hours of fun. She appeared on the doorstep with an agitated demeanour, and because of her morning hoarseness, they had to go over to her to hear the cause of her anxiety.

"Take the bridle off that donkey and let him out."

"Ah Granny, we're only goin' to have a little ride on him," said Paschal.

"That's all, Granny, an' he loves," pleaded Timmy, "we'll go real easy an' won't hurt 'em atall."

"Let that donkey out and don't ever catch him again …he's old like myself and needs rest."

The boys, with tears filling their eyes, released the donkey.

Robbie had just scored a goal and was jumping around the yard celebrating. The door opened and out ran Timmy; he was celebrating too.

"They're comin', they're comin' …c'mon, we'll go an meet 'em."

Paschal and Robbie rolled the 'goalposts' back into the haggard and followed Timmy down the lane in a skip and run, full of exuberance, joy and excitement.

BIKING HOME

Tom rolled his trousers tightly around his legs and pulled his long stockings up over them. The chain of his bike was very oily and if he wasn't careful, his trousers would be destroyed before he reached Wexford. The cloth shopping bag, with the few things for washing, hung on the handlebars, and he tied it around the neck of the bike to prevent it from getting caught in the spokes of the front wheel. From the big sprawling farmyard up to the main road was a short steep rise and he walked beside the bike, thinking and wondering if he had forgotten anything. He checked the inside pocket of his overcoat to make sure the money was still there. It was; his wages of two pound notes, a ten shilling note, and five shillings in coins.

He didn't mind the long journey home. Going through the city and the ferry crossing would make it feel shorter. Looking forward to seeing Molly, the children and his mother would shorten it too. He wondered how they were getting on, and if there were any problems or trouble. He prayed that everything would work out, but he couldn't be sure; the two women might be at war. His mother was contrary and headstrong, and Molly got all hot and bothered about little things; the poor children would be caught in the middle. It was a tough decision, a big upheaval for all of them. T'was lonely enough for him too, on his own in that big empty farmhouse all the week, but it must be worse for Molly trying to cope with everything on her own, a stranger in a strange place, with five children and a stubborn oul woman.

But it had to be done. When she gave him the little place and he gave her the promise that he would look after her to the end, he didn't think it would be so hard. Of course, if he could get a job near home, it would be much easier. Jobs are scarce around Wexford. You'd get one all right, but it would be hard to better the one he had with Mr Quinlivan. His mind swept back over the twenty years to when he first came to Waterford as a gangly eighteen-year-old. The five years he spent among the seeds and plants at Powers Nurseries was great, but the day he made that chance visit to Quinlivans meat shop for a pound of sausages, changed his life. He was so lucky that the owner happened to be behind the counter that day, and with no other customers, had time to start a little chat; an exchange that told Tom this was an important business man, and told Mr Quinlivan that he might be the man he was looking for. That set him up in a good job, first as a farm worker, and for the past ten years as farm manager. He felt proud that Mr Quinlivan placed so much trust in him. The big tillage farm on the rim of the city was nurtured and improved over the years, and he always felt proud when the boss praised him for working and managing it 'as if it was his own.'

The day was fine and the road into Waterford City was level all the way. As he cycled along at a leisurely pace, Tom's mind was busy planning on how to make the most of the little weekend break with Molly, his mother and the children. It would be all new and strange but he was determined to try and do everything to ease the worries, sort out any little problems, and try his best to make the whole thing work, especially for Molly and the children.

Navigating the maze of streets that led to the city centre was no problem to Tom. He was heading first to the big L&N shop in Broad Street. That was where his brother Peader was assistant manager, and he would get his usual special attention, and maybe a little extra value in his shopping. He parked the bike by the wall and made his way to the counter at the far end where Peader was looking like a film star with his clean-shaven face, his oil-slicked hair, the sparkling shirt and tie, and his snow white shop coat. Tom was used to seeing the elegance of his brother. Peader was the star of the family. Being the eldest, he had the sense to go along with his mother's wishes and stay in school. He had brains too, and used them to the full. That's what have him where he is to-day. Tom never felt a real brotherly closeness to Peader, although he always admired him. He was a good fellow but a little bit too prim and perfect.

"Are you on your way down now, Tom?" asked Peader, "God, it's a long way on a bike."

"I am, I just want a few things to bring with me."

"All right, what can I get you?"

A nice big lump of bacon, a parcel of rashers and sausages, and a pound of lovely country butter fitted neatly into the shopping bag, and when Tom was about to pay, Peader put his finger to his lips indicating silence, and that no payment would be required. Tom was really surprised, but pleased that he had found his brother in a unusually generous mood.

"I hope everything works out for you," said Peader, "tis not going to be easy; Mother is hard to manage."

"I know, but she's gone so shook now, she's softened a bit. If Molly can stick it for a while, it might work."

"But 'tis tough on you too, Tom, working and living on your own all the week, and then biking it down and back every weekend."

"I suppose it is. But sure, what can I do? If I could get a decent job down near home, t'would be better, but sure we'll see how it works out."

"Anyway, tell them all I was asking for them, and tell Mother I'll be down to see her when I get the chance."

"I will, and thanks for the things."

"Okay Boy. God be with you now, mind yourself."

The next stop was Hearne's on the Quay. They had everything from a needle to an anchor. Tom leaned his bike against the wall by the window. He wanted to keep an eye on the shopping bag as he entered the shop and approached the counter. Hearne's was the oldest hardware shop in Waterford, and if they hadn't what you wanted, they would get it for you. They also had plenty of long-serving staff and you were always attended to without delay.

"A dozen rabbit snares," said Tom, and the man quickly had them counted out and placed in a brown paper bag.

"That'll be one and nine pence, please."

Tom paid him, left the store, mounted the bike and headed along the quay in the direction of Wexford.

It was seven miles to Passage East where he would board the ferry that crossed the harbour to Ballyhack. That would leave him with another seven miles of narrow country roads, before arriving at the little thatched house, and reuniting with his loved ones. The road from

Waterford to Passage was level for halfway and downhill for the other half. Soon he was resting on the pier wall, waiting for the little ferryboat to return from Ballyhack. He was the only passenger on that crossing and with the bike slumped against the inside of the boat, and the engine at full rev, he sat and admired the picturesque expanse of Waterford Harbour. Soon old Padgie Byron was in full flow of non-stop conversation. Now in his seventies, he had operated the ferry for forty years since inheriting it from his late father. Losing his left leg from gangrene recently didn't bother him at all, and Tom marvelled at the way he handled the boat and moved around on crutches in his usual high spirits. Every passenger got a joke or two from Padgie, especially the new one relating to himself. As he lived in Passage East village, and his amputated leg was buried in Ballyhack graveyard, he would boast that he was the only man alive that had a leg at each side of the harbour.

The road out of Ballyhack was very hilly, dusty, and with lots of loose stones. Tom didn't make the same progress as he did on the other side. Still, as long as he didn't get a puncture and peddled at a good pace, he would make it home in about an hour.

ALL TOGETHER

The boys kept watch up in the little gable window. Taking turns, their eyes were on the railway gates in the distance and on the part of the lane that ran parallel with the railway line. Two hours of constant watch failed to ease their longing, and they were beginning to wonder was Daddy coming at all. Suddenly, a scream from Robbie signalled a sighting, and soon five children ran and skipped excitedly down the lane to escort their father home. Before he reached the house Tom had the happenings of the week, and he was very relieved to hear, that even with a few little hiccups, things had worked out fairly well.

Molly was at the door to welcome him home with a big smile and a loving embrace. Granny was in her seat beside a lovely red fire and she looked much better, but as usual, she was still complaining of the cough and the old bronchitis. Molly served tea and hot scones while Tom proudly emptied the shopping bag on the table and warmly related Peader's kind gesture.

"Oh that's great," said Molly, "but I can't believe it, he must have won the sweep or somethin'."

"Ah now, Mam, tha's not fair," countered Tom, "he's not the worst."

"How is Peader?" asked Granny.

"He's bloomin'; never better. He's dressed like a lord an' in great form."

"When is he coming down to see me?"

"He said to tell you he'll be down when he gets a chance."

"Ah sure, I know he's very busy. That's a very important job he has. He's a wonderful boy."

"He is," said Tom, unconvincingly.

Molly winked at her husband, but didn't comment.

26

After tea, Molly and the children brought Tom out to see the pony and trap. She couldn't find words strong enough to praise Johnny and Lizzie Moran for their kindness and generosity.

"They're the best in the world," said Tom, "you'll never be stuck for anything, with neighbours like them."

"Yeah," said Molly, and Johnny is so wonderful with the children."

"Ah sure, poor Johnny never grew up himself, he's still a big child."

"Oh now, they are just lovely; I can't thank them enough."

Paschal and Robbie insisted on showing their father how they could yoke the pony while Timmy stood in front of his head, holding his bridle. Soon a shuttle of pleasure trips up and down the lane had them all humming with delight until Tom said it was time to unyoke the pony, as he had another little adventure for them.

Reaching to his inside pocket, he took out the brown paper bag and the little coil of rabbit snares.

"What are them?" asked Timmy.

"Rabbit snares," shouted Paschal and Robbie together.

They had seen them with one of the workmen on the farm in Waterford.

"Would yis like rabbit soup?"

"We would, we would," they all answered in unison.

"Well, I'll show yis how to catch 'em, but first we have a bit of work to do before we can set the snares."

He led the children out to the field where he broke a branch from an ash tree, cut it into short lengths, pointed them at one end and explained that those would be the pegs that would secure the snares to the ground, holding the rabbit captive. He also cut short lengths of a light branch, about the thickness of a pencil, pointing one end and cutting a slit in the other end. These, he explained, would stand beside the rabbit path, holding the snare ring in position, keeping it upright and in line for the rabbit to run into it. In the car shed, they trimmed the pegs, fastened the snares to them, and prepared to set off on an exciting trip of adventure.

As the evening was getting dull and chilly, Tom and Molly persuaded Mina and Kenny to stay at home in the heat, and insisted on the three boys wrapping up well in caps and coats as they set out across the land to set the snares.

Reaching a big familiar field on the side of the hill, Tom told the boys that it was the field where he got most rabbits when he was snaring them in his youth. They walked around by the ditches, finding many paths and decided to set all the snares in that field.

Tom showed his sons how to set them, making sure the holding pegs were deep in the ground and the standing pegs held the rings at the correct height, and straight over the paths.

"When will the rabbits run into 'em?" asked Timmy.

"Tonight, I hope," replied his dad, "and we'll find them in the morn'"

"How many will we get?" asked Robbie.

"Oh now, I can't tell ye that, maybe a couple, if we're lucky."

When the last of the snares were set, Tom took a sweeping look around the entire field, making a note in his mind of the locations. He would need to find every snare in the morning in case any of them were knocked down. The boys were chatting and giggling with excitement and anticipation as they followed their father across the fields and lanes that led them back to the little thatched homestead.

Molly had a pot of stew boiling on the fire that was red hot from Kenny blowing the fan. It was so hot that Granny had to move back her chair and she chastised Kenny for not stopping when she told him.

The three older boys and their father arrived in, crowding the little kitchen.

"Oh, begor, that smells good," said Tom, "what is it?"

"I got a bit of boilin' beef in Campile yesterday, and I asked the butcher for all the bones he could give me. He gave me enough to make soup for the week," said Molly.

"Are we only gettin' bones and soup?" asked Robbie, "I'm really starvin."

"Ah, Robbie, don't be stupid," said Mina, "spuds an turnips are in it too; I peeled them with Mammy."

"Yeah, an' I blew the fan to boil 'em."

"You did, and you nearly blew the fire up the chimney," said Granny.

Molly lifted the lid of the pot and poked the spuds with a fork.

"Tis ready."

Tom lifted the pot off the crook and laid it down gently beside the table that was already set with bowls and spoons. They all sat in while Molly dished up the stew with a large mug. Granny had her meal by the fire.

"Ye won't have to buy any meat next week at all," said Paschal, addressing his mother.

"Why not?"

"Sure we'll have rabbits."

"Oh yeah," said Timmy, "an' we can make rabbit soup."

"I hope you're right," said his mother, "It'll help to spare the money."

They finished the stew. All said it was lovely except Granny, who left some beef. She said it was a bit tough for her false teeth.

Tom got up, got his old overcoat off the nail behind the door and put it on, telling the boys to come and wrap themselves up too.

"Where are we goin'?" asked Robbie.

"I have a little job for yis."

They went to the car shed, where Tom got an old bushman saw, and they headed out to the field. There, he cut down the overhanging branches of the ash trees that lined one side. The boys were thrilled to watch as the saw cut through and the branches crashed to the ground.

"Now," he said, "I'll cut 'em in small blocks an yis can bring 'em in to the shed."

The three boys filled their arms with as much as they could carry and began the trek in and out until all the cutting was done and one corner of the shed was piled up with lovely firewood. Timmy ran into the house and insisted on his mother coming out to see 'the great thing they had done.'

"Oh, that's great," she said, "we won't need near as much coal with them now."

"No Mammy," said Paschal, "an' t'will save more money."

Molly brought in some blocks and put them beside the fire. Granny reached down from her chair and took one up in her hands.

"Is he cutting the trees?"

Molly didn't reply.

"Those trees were planted by his father fifty years ago."

Molly eased her way to the door and beckoned Tom to come in. As he entered the kitchen, she silently pointed to Granny from behind her back. Granny heard him and swivelled slightly towards him.

"Are you cutting down the trees that your father planted?"

"No, I'm not, I only cut the branches that were hangin' out into the field."

"Don't cut any of them. When I'm gone you can do what you like."

'I'm tellin' you, Mother, I only cut the branches. It'll do the trees good, an' the field too."

"Well don't cut any more of them."

He didn't reply.

*

It was eight o'clock and the children had run out of things to tell their father about their first week in The Bogside. Molly placed the big galvanised iron bath in the middle of the kitchen. Tom took the pot of boiling water off the crane and emptied it into the bath. Cold water from the bucket was added, and with a block of carbolic soap thrown in, all was ready for the Saturday night wash.

Paschal and Robbie didn't get in as they had now outgrown the bath. Kneeling on the floor, they leaned in and washed their hands, heads and faces. The three younger ones took turns to submerge themselves in the sudsy water, emerging clean and refreshed, to be dried all over by their mother.

"Now" said Molly, "it's time for the Rosary."

The little kitchen was warm and cosy with a lovely fire of blocks and coal, and all except Granny knelt by the long forms. She sat in her chair by the fire gently fingering her well-worn black beads. Molly led the first mystery, Tom the second, and Granny the third. Paschal and Robbie led the fourth and fifth, and their mother then took over with the Hail Holy Queen, the Litany of the Blessed Virgin, and a long list of trimmings. Mina and Kenny were whispering to each other during much of the Rosary, but their mother overlooked it, knowing that they were bored and tired after a long day.

A pot of tea was made, and with the scones that Molly had baked earlier, provided a welcome night-cap for the children before they climbed the quaint little stairs that led to their beds. It was bedtime for Granny too. Molly had put the hot water bottle in the bed earlier and checked it again to see if it was hot enough. It was, and Granny shuffled her way to her room.

All was quiet in the little kitchen except for the hissing of the fresh timber blocks in the fire and the ticking of the clock on the mantelpiece. Tom pulled over a stool and sat at one side of the fire and Molly removed the cushions from Granny's armchair and sat in it at the other side. They chatted about the week that for both of them was a venture into the unknown. Tom didn't deny the loneliness he felt in the big empty farmhouse on his own, but his main concern was not for himself, but how Molly and the children were managing.

Molly let him know that she missed him too and wondered how long they would have to be apart. Only the future, which was uncertain at that point, could answer that. She related the happenings of the week, including the times when Granny irritated her, and she had to contain her anger in the interest of peace.

Getting the pony and trap was a God-send and made up for a lot, and she wanted Tom to know that all the children were so good – they couldn't be better and that helped a lot too.

Telling him about the school, she couldn't conceal her amazement at the way seven classes could be taught in that small building, and her admiration for Miss Harty for being able to run the school and teach all those classes on her own. Tom was well aware of all that as he had spent all his schooldays in that little building, and under the guidance of Miss Harty too. She was much younger then but was always a good and kind teacher.

They talked for two hours and Molly went over and gently opened the stairs door. She cocked her ear to listen and check for signs of little people awake upstairs, but all was quiet and peaceful. Tom locked the door, Molly made the fire safe and quenched the lamp, and both tip-toed up the stairs to their double bed on the loft, where Mina was sound asleep in her little bunk bed.

Having undressed, they got into bed, trying hard not to cause too much creaking in the old loose floor boards. The boy's room was only a plywood partition away and if any of them were awakened, it would spoil things.

Molly was overcome with the warmth of togetherness that was now restored between them, and knowing that it would be only temporary, she was determined to make the most of it. Tom was emotional too, and for a beautiful half hour in blissful tenderness, they managed to share an ecstasy without rattling the bed or disturbing the old floor boards.

*

A chill east wind blew across the bog and into the faces of Tom and his three sons as they set out on a rabbit-finding mission. It was only eight o'clock and being Sunday, they had to be back in time to get ready for Mass. Well wrapped and moving briskly, they didn't feel the cold except on their noses which soon turned red and began to leak.

They passed Moran's and continued along the rocky bog side lane, and climbed an old stile that took them into Mike Bannion's land. That was the foot of the hillside that looked out over the bog, and as they made their way up three big fields, they were soon blowing steam-like breaths into the freezing air. The top field, where the snares were set had a padlocked iron gate which the boys quickly climbed over. Their father paused on the highest bar and took a sweeping look across the entire field.

"Begor, we're in luck!"

The boys jumped and cheered.

"How many? How many?" shouted Robbie.

"Can I see 'em?" asked Paschal, as he climbed the gate again.

"Me too," screamed Timmy.

"Whisht, Whisht, don't make noise," said their father; "we'll go asy an' we won't frighten' 'em in case they jump and break the snares."

They went quietly to the first snare. A big rabbit was sitting, hunched up in a ball.

"Why is he sittin' like that?" whispered Robbie.

"He's bet out after strugglin' all night," his father answered.

"Ah, the poor little pet," said Timmy.

As they came closer the rabbit sprang into the air, frantically trying to escape. But held by the ground peg, all he could do was a mad circle that left a neat round patch of flattened grass.

Tom grabbed him by the hind legs.

"Begor, he's a fine big one."

'Will we bring him home alive?" asked Timmy.

"Ah no, we'll take him out of his misery now."

He told the boys to watch as he showed them how to kill a rabbit.

"Will it hurt 'em, Daddy?" asked Timmy.

"No, said his father, he won't feel a thing."

They watched wide-eyed as he held him in a hanging position in his left hand, and with his right hand wide open, he gave him a sharp chop on the neck, just behind the ears. Without a struggle or a murmur, the rabbit was dead.

"That's easy," said Robbie.

"Yeah, I could do that," said Paschal.

Two more rabbits were captured and Tom let Paschal put the third one to sleep.

"Now, yis'll know how to do it when I'm not here."

"I will, 'tis easy, thanks for showin' me."

"Can I do wan too?" asked Robbie.

"Yeah, maybe next weekend, Robbie, if we get any."

Tom took up the snares. He knew the boys wouldn't be able to travel the fields before school in the mornings. They could set them again next weekend.

Carrying a rabbit each, the boys followed their father down the hilly fields, oblivious to the biting wind, their hearts thumping with the sheer joy of adventure.

On their way past Moran's farmyard, they saw Johnny approaching the exit to the lane, pushing a loaded wheelbarrow. Startled, he stopped suddenly and straightened up.

"Christ God, who have we?"

Tom and the boys were so wrapped up with coats, scarves and caps that they weren't immediately recognisable.

"Oh sure 'tis you, Tom, and the chaps …what way a yis atall?"

"Ah sure we're grand, Johnny …how is yerself an' the mother?"

"Couldn't be better, Tom. Christ God! yis have rabbits too …where did yis get 'em?"

"Up in Mike Bannion's top field," said Tom, "there's plenty of 'em around."

"Christ God! Sure the place is full of 'em …will yis ate them now?"

"We will," said Robbie.

"An' we'll have rabbit soup too," said Timmy.

"Begob, that's powerful altogether …that'll make big men o' yis."

Tom glanced at the contents of the wheelbarrow and saw a dead, new-born calf, with a white head, still wet and slimy.

"Did ye have a bit o' bad luck, Johnny?"

"Christ God, I did …dead born …a bloody young heifer that shouldn't be in calf atall, atall."

"What happened?"

"Sure didn't she break into Mike Bannion's cattle last summer, an' a yearlin' bull done the job."

"An' did ye know she was in calf?"

"Know! I hadn't an idea until she started springin' …an' then she wasn't able to calf …tryin' all night …only for I found 'er this morn' in the haggard an' managed to pull out the calf, she'd be dead herself."

"An' how is she now?"

"Oh she's tip top ..after gettin' up an' all …now I'll have te milk the little fecker …I'll make a hole across in the bog for this one first."

'Well, Johnny, I'm sorry ye had that bit o' trouble …we'll keep goin' an' let ye do yer work."

"Ah sure Tom, as the fella said, God send us no bigger loss."

They moved on and Johnny pushed the wheelbarrow across the lane. At the small wooden gate that led into the bog he turned and called after them.

'Oh Tom! I'll be goin' to second Mass an' if yis want a lift I'll bring yis."

Tom swivelled back.

"Oh, thanks Johnny, but sure we wouldn't all fit in."

"Christ God sure me mother don't go atall, an' I'll have an empty motor car …I'll stuff yis in somewhere."

"I'll tell ye wha', Johnny …Molly an' the kids can go with you an' I'll go on the bike."

'Couldn't be better, Tom …I'll give the horn a blow at the gate."

'Thanks Johnny."

"Thanks Johnny," the three boys said in unison.

The old black Ford Prefect was laden down with Johnny and Molly in the front and five children in the back. He drove slowly down the lane trying to dodge the deepest potholes, but the car still jerked and swayed, adding to the fascination and fun for the children as they merrily swayed over and back as if they were in a boat on a stormy sea. Johnny wasn't enjoying the fun.

"Christ God, will yis stay quiet there in the back or yis'll turn over the motor car …we'll all end up in the dike."

Suddenly there was stillness and silence in the back as Johnny negotiated the rest of the bouncy lane, passed through the railway gates and on to the road stretching three miles to the little church on the hill.

They passed a lot of bikers and a few ponies and traps. Johnny knew them all and gave Molly their names and a little bit of information about them all. They came up behind a white pony and cart that was holding the middle of the road and Johnny hadn't room to get by. A big stout man with a black overcoat and hat was kneeling in the middle of the cart and two women sitting with their legs dangling from each side lace.

"Why won't he keep in?" asked Molly.

Johnny blew the horn a couple of times.

"That's 'The Deaf Sutton'; he's a contrary oul fecker. He was never in time for Mass in his life, an' he wants to keep everyone else late as well."

"Is that his family with him?"

"Yeah, that's his wife an' daughter."

"You'd think they'd get him to go early."

'Sure the priest himself can't get any good of 'em. He'd be in the sacristy all togged out with the boys ready to go out on the alter to say Mass, an' he'd be watchin' through the window where he could see up along the road to Andy Ronan's forge. When the white pony would come around the corner he'd say to the alter boys: "We can go now lads, 'The Deaf' is comin'."

Molly was still laughing when, having passed 'The Deaf' and his family, they overtook Tom, who was wheeling his bike up the yellow hill. Johnny blew the horn a few times, Molly waved and smiled warmly, and the children in the back all waved and shouted. Looking back through the rear window they saw him reach the brow of the hill, throw his leg over the bike and peddle on after them.

As the motor car swung around the wide area in front of the church, little groups of people were chatting, waiting for the time to go in. They all seemed to stretch and strain to get a good look inside the car and identify the passengers.

"Christ God," exclaimed Johnny, they'll think I have a new woman."

"Aye," said Molly laughing, "an' a motor car full o' children."

"Oh Jasus, how am I goin' to explain mesef atall, atall."

'Don't mind 'em, Johnny …they're only jealous of ye."

"'Tis true for ye, Missis; say nothin', that'll fix 'em."

Father Donovan gave a long sermon about the sixth commandment, rambling on for over half an hour on the correct behaviour between a man and a woman before marriage, and in married life. He became heated at times and banged the pulpit a few times with his fist. Molly noticed people shifting in their seats and uneasy, and wondered what the children would make of it. On the journey home, she asked Johnny what he thought of the sermon.

"Christ God, I never heard the batin' of it …ye'd swear he was married all his life, with a house full a children."

Molly laughed.

"Your right, Johnny …they think they're all saints, an' know everything about everybody … tryin' to frighten us they are."

Almost home again, they crossed the railway line and zig zagged along the rugged lane with the little thatched homestead looming larger in view. Rounding the bend, Johnny failed to avoid two very deep potholes and the underside of the car scraped against the raised centre of the lane. The engine suddenly erupted in a loud roaring noise.

"Christ God, the bloody exhaust pipe is broke."

"Oh, Johnny, I'm awful sorry," said Molly, as the children stared wide-eyed in the back. "We were too big a load."

"Not atall, Missis, that oul pipe was wore out …I knew t'was ready to break …I'll fix it in the afternoon."

He tied it with wire and Molly and the children walked the short distance to the house.

When Tom arrived home, Molly had the rashers and sausages sizzling on the pan. Granny said she liked the smell although it was years since she made a fry herself. A loaf of bread was sliced up and fried with a half dozen eggs and all sat in for a rare treat, with the compliments of the L&N and Peader. Soon the plates were licked clean and not a crumb left. Even Granny finished her's, and Molly helped her wipe the grease off her chin.

Tom said he would bring the boys to show them the shortcut to school through the fields, and Molly told the boys to wear their coats and caps as they would be cold after leaving the warm kitchen.

Having passed Moran's they climbed a low stone wall and went up the hill through three fields of Mike Bannion's farm. At the far end of the third field they climbed over an iron gate that led on to an old disused lane with overgrown hedges. They walked in single file on the centre path to a clearing, where another lane crossed from right to left, and turning right to walk another short distance, they were soon out on the road that would take them the final mile and a half to the school.

It was a steady climb most of the way but would be all down hill on their way home. The three boys would be on their own until they met the road, but they would then meet with Dicksy Kelly's two boys and Joiner Curran's three girls.

"Daddy," said Robbie, did you go this way to school?"

"Begor I did, Robbie, for six years."

"An', who went with ye?" asked Timmy.

"Oh sure, there was five of us …Peader, Tim, Agnes, Mary an' meself."

"An' yis all walked for six years? said Paschal.

'We did, an' most of the year we went in our bare feet."

"Why?" asked Timmy, "did yis have no boots?"

'Oh, we had, but we had to save 'em for Sundays an' the winter …nearly everyone was the same."

They arrived back at the lane beside Moran's and Tom asked them were they sure they knew the way. They looked at one another and all answered "Yes."

When they arrived home, Molly was airing Tom's working clothes before packing them in the bag for his return to Waterford.

"Will three pairs of socks be enough?" she asked.

"Deed it will; I can wash a pair meself if I want to."

"Y'ill soon have to go; t'will be late when ye get back."

"Ah, t'won't be too bad if I can get the oul ferry quick."

The children all looked thoughtful and quiet. Molly knew how much they would love for their father to stay at home and not be gone for a whole week. Timmy's eyes welled up with tears and Robbie stared at the floor to avoid eye contact.

"I have one more job to do before I go," Tom said with a smile on his face.

They all perked up.

"Did yis forget?"

"Forget what?" asked Paschal.

"The rabbits!"

"Oh, God Yeah," said Molly, "I forgot all about 'em."

The boys and their father went out to the shed where the rabbits were hanging stiff from the rafters. They had been panched and cleaned out before they were hung up and Tom showed the boys how to skin them.

"It's very simple, if ye start right," he said.

Peeling from the hind legs to the head, he soon had three skinless rabbits ready for the pot.

Molly placed them in a big basin of water and soon the gloomy focus turned again to Daddy's departure.

The children and their mother went with him down the lane to the railway gates. Kenny sat on the carrier of the bike, holding on to the saddle as his father walked beside him wheeling it. The evening was blustery and cold, but Tom didn't expect any rain before he reached Waterford.

Molly walked close to him so that they could talk quietly, without the older children hearing.

"I'll miss ye now when yer gone."

"Ah, I know, but sure I'll see ye next Saturday."

"That's a long time."

"Ah, t'won't be long goin'."

"A lot can happen between now an' then."

'I know, but sure what can we do?"

She took his left hand in hers and squeezed it. Their eyes met. Nothing more was said.

At the gates he lifted Kenny from the bike and gave him a hug and a kiss. Mina quickly ran over to him for her share. She opened her arms and he bent down with a hug and a kiss for her too. The other three boys had outgrown hugs and kisses and, pretending to be big and brave, stood with their hands in their pockets. But Molly saw that Timmy was losing the battle to be brave. His eyes were overflowing, and she took him by the hand to his father for a parting hug. She then gave Tom a hug and a kiss herself, and to a chorus of goodbyes and much vigorous waving, he threw his leg over the saddle and peddled away.

Not much was said on the way back. Molly carried Kenny when he got tired walking, but her mind was in deep thought. This can't continue. They would never get used to this. It wasn't fair on the children. It wasn't fair on Tom, and it wasn't fair on her. Looking at the five children, she knew that they were all missing him terribly, especially the older boys. They would now have to face that long journey to school every day through the oul fields and come home in the evening and not see their father from one end of the week to the other. Poor Tom would have to face that oul empty house, and that long trek up and down every weekend after his hard week's work. No, it couldn't work. It wouldn't work, and sooner or later it would end in tears.

A steely determination lurked behind her gloom. This was a problem that she would solve, whatever it took to do it.

The easy way was for Tom to get a job near here, so that he would be home every night. Even if they had to do with less money, they would make ends meet someway. But Tom loved that job in Waterford. It made him proud to be a farm manager. He felt it was an important job. Maybe not as important as Peader's, but it made him happy and contented. He wouldn't get a job like that down here, but anything would be better than the way things were now.

They rounded the corner and the old thatched house came starkly into view. Nothing about it was appealing . It looked forlorn and forbidding. Goin' back in there without Tom and facing that cantankerous oul one was tough. She was a time bomb that could explode anytime, especially when Tom wouldn't be there. With a heavy heart she led the children up the short, grassy lane and into the little house.

Nellie and Larry

It was a frosty Wednesday morning, and Molly's face felt the biting north east wind as she walked briskly over the lane to collect the milk at Moran's. The poor children, she thought, had to face that an hour earlier. Their little hands and feet must have been frozen. Miss Harty would probably have a good fire in the school, warm them up, keep them from getting a flu.

Before she left the house she had made Granny snug by the fire, and left Mina and Kenny happily playing with their little toys.

She entered Moran's yard.

"What a ye doin' out in the cowld, Missis? That frosty wind'ed cut the face off ye."

'Oh Johnny, ye gave me a start …sure I had to come over for the milk."

He was in the cow-house, sitting on a small three-legged stool, milking a cow into a galvanise bucket which was half full of milk. Two big red and white cows and one small black and white heifer stood in their stalls chewing their cud.

"Are they milkin' well, Johnny?"

"Christ God, these two are milkin' powerful, but that little bitch over there is lucky to be alive."

"Oh yeah, Tom told me …is that her now?"

"That's her now …she was lucky I found 'er tryin' to calve."

"She looks grand now"

"Oh, she'll make a right little cow, but sure she was too young to go in-calf, an' she no more than a calf 'erself."

"Did ye milk 'er yet?"

'Christ God I did …she have a power a milk …an' she's as quiet as a mouse."

41

"Oh, she's lovely, Johnny; good luck with her."

'Well, I'll tell ye now, Missis, she's a bloody nuisance to me …no calf to put on 'er, an' havin' te milk 'er twice a day …I'd sell 'er if I could, only she's too small."

'God Johnny, I'd buy 'er meself if I thought I could manage 'er."

He rose from under the cow and straightened up.

"Christ God! A powerful idea …sure why wouldn't ye manage 'er … there's not a kick in the world in 'er."

"How much would ye be lookin for 'er?"

He lifted his old cloth cap, scratched his head, and backed to the wall to get a good look at her again.

'Jasus, sure she's not worth a whole lot now 'till she grows up … about twelve quid would be as much as I'd get for 'er"

"That's not much for a cow, Johnny."

"'Tis not, but sure ye couldn't call 'er a cow yet … I'll tell ye what I'll do with ye now Missis … ten quid an' she's yours …an' ye can bring 'er over an' pay me whenever ye have it."

"Oh Johnny … are ye sure? … I will buy 'er …Tom an' the chaps will get 'er on Saturday an' pay ye an' all …we have a few pounds saved."

"Couldn't be better! Howld out yer hand there."

He clinched the deal with a slap of his milky hand on hers.

"Christ God! Tha's ra'ly powerful now."

Her step was light and bouncy on the way back. The sharp wind was behind her and she felt upbeat and enthused by her little purchase. The old cow house would now come in handy, she would have lots of milk, and could even make her own butter. That little heifer would grow into a lovely cow and have a calf every year. That was a great mornin's work, a real stroke of luck. Poor Johnny was annoyed at what had happened to his heifer, but now *he's* happy too. The oul sayin' is true: "'Tis an ill wind that don't blow in somebody's favour.'

Humming to herself, and with a new feeling of optimism, she skipped up the grassy lane, lifted the latch and entered the little thatched house.

In the kitchen, she immediately smelled trouble. Mina and Kenny were sitting at the table, their faces flushed from crying. They jumped down and ran to her.

"What's wrong? What happened?"

"Granny took our toys," cried Kenny.

"An she made us stay sittin' at the table," added Mina.

Granny swivelled around.

"What kept you so long?…Gossiping, I suppose …and I trying to control those little brats."

"Oh, Granny, sure I wasn't that long …what were they doin'? …I left them playin' with their toys."

"Playing! Fighting and bawling and making noise …you know I'm not able for that now."

"Alright, I'm sorry if they annoyed ye …it won't happen again."

She wiped their faces, wrapped them in their coats and caps, and took them by the hands out the door. In the car shed, she got the pony's bridle.

"What are we goin' to do," asked Mina.

"We're goin' te yoke the pony an' clear away somewhere out of here."

Well wrapped up and with a rug around them in the trap, Molly and the two children drove down the lane, across the railway line and on to the main road. The pony, trotting evenly, was soon blowing foggy puffs of breath into the freezing air. The children, with their buttoned-up coats, gloves and pixies were warm, happy, and fully recovered from their distress. Their mother, still flushed with annoyance and frustration, was hoping her sister would be at home when they arrived at her house in Ballycullane.

The journey of about five miles gave Molly plenty of time for thought. It took them over hilly countryside, and while the pony drummed out a nice steady rhythm with his trotting on the level, the burden of the trap, a heavy woman and two children, slowed him to a walk up the hills. Once over the brow and facing down hill again, he wanted to take off, and had to be restrained from speeding up to a gallop, as the loaded trap began to push him on.

The children were enjoying it, admiring the animals in the frost-covered fields, and the many and varied farmhouses they passed. Molly's form was improving too, feeling a bit more relaxed, and looking forward to seeing her sister. It was a year since she last saw Nellie, and although she had told her in a letter at Christmas that she was coming to The Bogside in late January, she would be shocked to see her arrive at her doorstep out of the blue.

Nellie, the youngest of them all and the real character of the family, was always her favourite. She had a heart of gold. Though funny and light-hearted, she was still the one that worried about everything, fussed about everyone, and never bothered about herself, her own wellbeing or her appearance. The only real argument they ever had was about fags. She'd smoke the leg off a pot, and they were ruining her health and her looks. But the argument was lost; she smoked on.

Molly felt good to live now within visiting distance of her after all those years, and even though she hadn't planned the trip so soon, until it was forced on her, she was glad to use it as a comfort and an escape. Whatever depression or worry she ever had, she was always better after a chat and a laugh with Nellie.

Passing through Blakestown crossroads, Molly could see the children getting a little weary and told them that they had only another half a mile to go. The road ahead was smooth and level and with the pony trotting evenly, they were at Nellie's gate in a few minutes.

It was a County Council cottage, on a bend in the road, with two large piers and an iron entrance gate. It hadn't changed over the years – still the grey walls, white sash windows with faded lace curtains, and the little yard in front, covered with gravel. The gate was painted a bright red, and the front door, with it's little slated apex canopy, was also red, but not as startling as the gate.

With the pony breathing heavily and his face touching the gate, Molly stood up in the trap, stretched her neck and listened. The children were wide-eyed too; they had never been there before. The sound of clucking hens and the odd crow of a rooster was coming from behind the house.

"Hello! Nellie! Hello" She shouted as loud as she could, but there was no answer. A thick plume of black smoke rose from the chimney and Molly felt sure that there was someone in the house. She shouted again. The door opened suddenly. Nellie appeared. She seemed a bit startled and bewildered. Looking her usual motherly self in a loose red cardigan over a black skirt, she looked good except for a few extra lines in the face and a grey tint running through her bobbed dark hair.

She ventured forward and recognising her sister, threw her hands in the air, opened her eyes and mouth wide and exclaimed: "Oh Jasus, Mary an' Joseph, 'tis you Molly …Where did ye come from atall? An two lovely children, God bless 'em …come in, come in …wait 'till I open the gate for ye …Larry! Come out here 'till ye see whose here."

Larry puffed his way out, looking feeble and breathless.

Molly drove into the yard, got out and was warmly embraced by Nellie. The children got a big hug too. The pony was unyoked from the trap, tied to the gate, but the tackling wasn't removed. They went inside to the little snug kitchen, neat and tidy with a flagstone floor, flowery wallpaper and a red turf fire.

"You're lookin' very well, Nellie, an *you're* not lookin' too bad either, Larry."

"Oh Molly melanna, don't be talkin'. Sure I'm not too bad atall, but that poor crater over there is crawkin' the whole time …he haven't a breath …there's times yid hear'm wheezin' in Enniscorthy."

Larry was back in his chair at the fire. He had put on a lot of weight, especially around the waist, and being very low-sized, it was making him even more breathless. Molly felt for him; she remembered him as a steam roller driver for the County Council, a great breadwinner until he got that bloody asthma.

"Ah sure, I'll never be any better now, Molly, I'm headen for the long box."

Nellie swivelled around.

"Jasus Larry; don't be talkin' like that! Wha' would I do then?"

"Get another one, a course! Wha' else would ye do?"

"Oh n troth n I wouldn't …where would I get another one like you?"

"That'll do ye now. What d'*you* say, Molly, amn't I right?"

"Ah now, Larry, you're not goin' to snuff it for a long time yet." said Molly. She always enjoyed this banter between them.

Nellie, crossing the floor, stopped to address both of them.

'Oh, Curse o' God on the snuff …he have it too good there, roastin' his arse at the fire every day, an' I dancin' attendance on 'em."

Molly never doubted Nellie for a good punch line to end an exchange. "Are the twins at school?"

"Begor they are," said Nellie, "the poor little divils have to walk nearly two miles every morn' an' evenin' in this cowld weather …sit in there at the table an' ye can be tellin' me the news while I'm makin' the tay …when did ye come?"

We're there nearly a couple a weeks now …Tom is still workin' away in Waterford an' the three chaps are in school."

"Well, d'ye know what, Molly? I never thought yid do it …T'was an awful big move …how are things goin'?"

"Te tell ye the truth, I didn't think I'd do it meself …T'was Tom that got the better of me."

"An' how is herself?"

"Oh, there's not a bit o' fear of her, crooked and contrary as ever …she'd ait the face off ye for nothin'."

Christ Molly girl, how in the name a Jasus are ye goin' te manage 'er?"

"T'wont be asy, that's for sure …But sure I knew that all the time."

"What age is she now?"

"She'll be eighty on the first of August, an I suppose the house'll be full for that …nuns, priests an' God knows who else."

"Oh, damn it aye, the nuns …sure I forgot. Eighty! An' she still givin' out …an' ye know, Molly, the like of that oul one could see the hundred!"

"Ah, she won't …she's gone shook …Tom says she's gone down hill quick lately."

"Well, God forgive me for sayin' it, but the quicker the better, for your sake."

The table was set, the tea was ready, and a big Christmas cake was placed in the centre.

"Start at it now lads," said Nellie, as she cut big slices for the children. "d'yis like sweet cake?"

"I do," said Mina.

"An' I do too," whispered Kenny.

That's the last o' Christmas now; I only made two this year."

"You're as good as ever at 'em," said Molly, ready to savour a large square.

"Ah sure musha, I donna …there's no one mad about sweet cake in this house …I'll wrap up half o' that for ye te bring home te the poor little chaps."

"Oh God, thanks Nellie; they'll be delighted … them are the boys'd scoff it in no time."

After the tea Molly helped with the tidying up. Nellie gave the children a few little toys to play with, and the adults sat around the fire chatting.

"God Molly, it must be an awful change for ye to be over there in the back o' beyond an' ye so used te Waterford."

"Oh sure i'tis …but the Moran's are very good te me …they fixed me up with the pony an' trap, an' 'tis a God-send …I'd be stuck on'y for 'em."

"An poor oul Tom," said Larry, "he must be lonesome all the week on his own too."

"Oh troth n he's not," said Nellie, with a smirk on her face, "I bet ye he have a young one …no shortage o' them in Waterford."

Molly laughed. "Tom with a young one? That'll be the day."

"If he could get a middlin' job near home, twould be better for the whole lot o' yis," said Larry.

'This now ye said it, Larry, but sure the job he'd get down here with some oul farmer wouldn't be much good."

"Jasus Molly," said Nellie, "'tis the truest word ye ever said. Them bloody farmers wouldn't give ye the steam off their piss."

"Ah now," said Larry, "they're not all as bad as that …even if the wages was a bit less than he have now, it might be a damn sight better than traipsin' up an' down that journey every week."

"Larry! Don't be talkin' through yer arse, said Nellie seriously …the woman have five children te feed an clothe …we have ony two, an' we can't make ends meet …d'ye know what, Molly, I didn't get a bit a mate for the last week."

Larry straightened up.

"Oh, ye didn't? Why, is mine fish or wha'?"

Molly laughed heartily. Larry's laugh started a fit of coughing. Nellie wasn't amused.

'Com'on Molly till I show ye the fowl."

The children followed them out the back door into the little enclosed yard. It was stone-paved, but wet and greasy from the hens.

"God Nellie, ye have a lot of 'em …they must ate a lot."

"Ate! They'd ate ye out o' house an' home …I have te get rid of half of 'em …Jasus Molly; d'ye want a few hens? …they're nearly all layin', an' sure a few eggs'd crown the children."

"Are ye sure, Nellie? God t'would be great, but I wouldn't want 'em for nothin'; I'd pay ye."

'Musha Molly melanna, don't be foolish …bring a half dozen with ye an' bring that oul cluckin' wan too, an' she'll hatch for ye."

They hushed them into the little henhouse and Nellie went back into the house for some strips of old clothing to tie the legs. The children laughed and clapped as each hen was tackled and held by Nellie while Molly did the fettering.

"Will they bite our legs in the trap?" asked Mina.

"Oh Jasus," exclaimed Nellie, "I forgot that …hould on there now."

She got two old jute bags from the shed, packed the hens into them, and tied each bag with string.

"Now," she said, 'the feckers can't bite …but I hope they won't smother."

The two women chatted in the shed while the children played around the grassy half acre. Nellie got out the fags, had a good smoke, and Molly pretended not to notice.

"Any account of the rest o' the lads? asked Molly.

"D'ye know what, girl, I didn't see one o' them for ages …sure ye see yerself now the way I'm fixed …I'm anchored with that poor oul invalid inside …where can I go? He could be dead when I'd come back."

"*I'll* have te go see 'em soon now" said Molly, "or I'll never live it down."

'I was over in Haggard before Christmas, said Nellie, "an' they were all grand then, but I wasn't up in Aclare te see Nan for ages …I suppose their alright or I'd have heard."

"T'will have to be a Sunday for Haggard, I suppose, with Nicky workin' all the week, but sure any day'd do te go see Nan; she's always there."

"Aye, poor Nan seldom stirs out …did ye have any word from Aggie in London?"

"Oh, I did," said Molly, "she sent a parcel of clothes for Christmas …t'was a God-send …on'y for 'er I don't know what we'd do."

"She's a jingler," said Nellie, "always was …I hope the poor crater comes home in the summer; I'd love te see 'er."

"Ah, I'd say she'll be home this year all right … the girls are gettin' big with 'er now an' t'would be 'asier to travel."

They moved back inside. Larry was smoking, coughing and wheezing.

"Curse o' God on them fags, they're killin' ye," said Nellie, "the doctor might as well be talkin' te the wall."

"D'ye hear that one talkin', an' she'd smoke the cross off an ass."

Molly laughed, but didn't comment.

"Get in there Molly te the fire an' warm yerself yer own way before ye go."

Larry moved over a little and turned the fan wheel. Molly and the children got heated up for the road. The glowing red fire soon had their faces flushed and they stood up and Molly made a move to go.

"Don't be long 'till ye come again," said Larry.

"I won't … I'll see ye soon … an' I hope y'ill be better then."

"Well, if I don't, I won't be here atall … I'll be after kickin' the bucket."

'Ah, ye won't … good luck 'till I see ye again."

"Good luck, Molly girl, an' safe home."

Nellie helped to yoke the pony. They loaded the two sacks of hens into the hold of the trap, leaving barely enough room for the legs. The hens were all silent except for the hatching one; she was still clucking. Nellie held the gate open while Molly manoeuvred the pony and trap around.

"Well, God Almighty bless yis for comin' an' I hope yis'll come soon again."

"I'll see ye soon, Nellie …an' thanks for the hens."

"Oh, don't mention it, girl … ye can get more the next time …I hope y'ill be able te manage that oul one now … don't let 'er best ye … God be with ye … an' safe home."

"I won't … gw'in out o' the cowld …y'ill get yer death."

As the pony found the rhythm of the trot, Molly and the children looked back to see Nellie perched in the middle of the road with both arms in the air waving vigorously.

Prayers Answered

Molly relaxed and reflected for as long as she could before getting out of bed. She had hoped to lie on for an extra while but all the children were up early, running around and celebrating the fact that it was Saturday, that there was no school, and that their Daddy would be coming home in the afternoon.

When she crossed to the little gable window for a look out at the weather, she was pleasantly surprised to see a clear sky, a hazy sun peeping over the horizon, and the entire stretch of the bog looking clearer and more cheerful than she had ever seen it.

She straightened the blankets and the quilt on the bed and a spark ignited inside her when she thought of Tom and herself reunited in there again to-night. She had really missed him in the past week.

At the table, they filled their bellies with hot porridge, tea and fresh wheaten bread and butter.

"Oh God I'm so stuffed," said Paschal, "I can't move."

"So am I," said Robbie.

"Well, yis'll have te move quick now 'cause we have te get that cow house ready before yer father comes home."

Molly had worked at the hen house herself while the boys were in school, but she left the cow house until they were all there.

"Hurry on now," she said, "Granny'll soon be up an' I don't want yis under 'er feet when she comes."

Out in the yard, Molly said she'd chance letting out the hens. They were kept in since she got them and she hoped that they wouldn't stray away. When she opened the door they rushed out, all except the clucking one. She was content to sit snug and happy in the orange box that Molly had placed in the corner for laying. She resented being disturbed and tried picking the hands lifting her out. But out she went and the children were delighted to find three lovely brown eggs in the nest.

"D'yis know what we'll do lads," said Molly, 'we'll collect a dozen eggs and set 'er ... sure she'd be a damn sight better hatchin' out a clutch o' chickens than cluckin' around the place like she is now."

The children were delighted.

"How long will she be lyin' on 'em for the chickens te come out?" enquired Timmy.

"About three weeks."

"Oh Mammy, can I have one?" asked Mina.

"Me too! Me too!" said Kenny, "I want a little one."

"If they all come out, they'll be enough for everyone," said their mother.

"An' when they get big, what will we do with 'em?" asked Robbie.

"We'll ate 'em," said Paschal, an' we'll have lovely chicken soup."

"Ah now lads," said their mother, "ye know ye should never count yer chickens before they're hatched."

She gave the big boys a job each in the cow house. It hadn't been stirred for years, covered with cobwebs, loose stones having fallen out of the walls, some sheets loose on the roof, and the stone floor covered in a thick crust of cow dung.

"I have te go in now te fix up Granny, an' you's work away ... good boys; work hard now; won't yis ... an whatever yis do, don't let on te Granny what yis are at."

"We'll work hard," said Timmy, " Daddy won't know it when he comes."

Molly hadn't mentioned a thing about the heifer to Granny all the week. She was afraid of her reaction. That flare-up the other morning created a bad atmosphere that has been there ever since. She couldn't stop her from getting the heifer, but she might object to the old cow house being touched. Tom would sort all that out with her when he comes; she won't best *him*. She thought again about the gift it would be if Tom could be there with her all the time instead of being away in Waterford. That oul one wouldn't get all her own way if he was here. She prayed silently to the Blessed Mother to solve the problem somehow; if not, she didn't know what would happen.

When she joined them again in the cow house, she was delighted with the work they had done. After another hour's work the whole job was completed. Molly stood back to admire it and looked up.

"Oh, the sheets on the roof! We nearly forgot 'em … get the hammer out o' the shed, Paschal, an' ye might be able te get up an' tighten 'em."

With the old lump hammer under his arm, he climbed the stone ditch that was alongside and scrambled up on to the low side of the roof. The nails on two of the corrugated sheets had become loose and he began hammering them back in. In a lull between the hammering, the hoarse voice of Granny was heard, and looking across, he was frozen to see her on the doorstep thrashing her hands in the air and frothing out of the mouth.

"Get down! Get down! You'll knock down my cow house! Get down and stop that hammering!"

Molly was inside the cow house with the other children, warning them with her finger to her lips not to make a stir. Paschal gingerly climbed down. She turned and went back in.

It was mid-afternoon when Timmy, on duty up at the gable window, spotted his father biking it along the lower lane. A stampede followed and he was escorted home with lots of loud chatter and mouthfuls of news.

But they had agreed on Paschal's insistence that they would not tell him about the heifer or the hens. They would wait until he arrived in the yard and see for himself the hens, the new hen house, and the great work they had all done on the cow house.

As he wheeled the bike up the grassy lane into the yard he was met by cockling hens scattering out of his way. Molly was there to meet him, embraced him warmly, explained about the hens, and ushered him towards the cow house.

"Wha's goin' on here?" he exclaimed.

"We're gettin' a new cow," Robbie couldn't contain his excitement any longer.

Timmy couldn't either. "Ye, an' we'll have our own milk an' every-thin'."

Mina was not to be left out. 'An', Daddy, she'll have a little calf ev'y year too."

Tom looked enquiringly at Molly, now smiling and enjoying his bewilderment. She told him the whole story.

"Begor, tha's powerful altogether ... a few pigs now an we'll be right as rain."

She then told him about the row with Granny when she came back from Moran's, how she had to clear off to Nellie's to avoid a bigger row, and that hardly a word had passed between them since.

"She ruined the whole week on us."

"Oh Ah." He pursed his lips tightly.

"Tom, you'll have to do somethin' ...will ye talk to 'er ... no one could stick that ... I'll be gone mental if that keeps up."

"I will. I will. I'll tell 'er ... we'll sort it out."

"Well, ye know now anyway, Tom, an' you're the on'y one that can get any good of 'er."

They went inside and Molly lifted the lid on the pot of rabbit stew that was simmering on the fire. It was nearly ready.

"You're home early, Tom, did you see Peader?" Granny had swivelled around to get a full view of him.

"No, I didn't go near 'em atall ... I didn't want te be puttin' on 'em every week ... I came straight down."

'You should have went in to see him ... I do be thinking about him."

" Oh, he's alright ... no fear o' him."

'Tom, you'd want to talk to them chaps of yours; they're as wild as goats."

"Ah, sure, all chaps are like that ...t'would be worse if they were sick or sometin'."

"Sick! They're as hardy as snipes on the bog ... nothing would do them to-day only up on the roof of the old cow house hammering the life out of it and it ready to fall down."

"Divil a fall ... sure they're after doin' it up ... a whole new job ... ready for the cow."

'What cow?"

"We're gettin' a heifer off Moran's ... sure she'll crown us."

"And who'll milk her?"

"Molly"

"Ah, don't be foolish ...how can she do everything? ... You'll have to come home and get a job around here."

"I would if I could."

He lifted the pot off the crane and Molly dished out the stew.

With full bellies and the light through the little window fading, Tom and the children rose from the table. The heifer had to be brought over from Moran's, and that had to be done before dark. The boys got their coats and caps.

"Can I go too, Mammy," asked Mina.

'An' me too, Mammy," pleaded Kenny.

"Ah no, let the big lads go … yis'd be perished with the cowld … yis'll see the heifer when she comes."

Molly gave a wink to Tom as she passed him on her way upstairs. From underneath the mattress she pulled out a wallet. Holding it tenderly she raised it to her face. She loved that old wallet, the soft feel of it, the pure leather smell of it, but especially because she had it for over twenty years, since the family got together and bought it for her twenty-first birthday. It was lucky too. Funds were often low over the years but it was never completely empty. She withdrew ten pounds from the thirty-five it contained, closed it carefully, and replaced it again under the mattress.

When she returned to the kitchen, she slipped the ten pound note into Tom's hand, and he gave her the two pounds wages, keeping ten shillings for himself to pay the ferry and keep him for the week ahead. They were ready to go.

"Molly saw them out to the little hall.

"Will yis have a job gettin' 'er over?"

"Ah, hardly, sure we have plenty help."

"Johnny says she's as quiet as a lamb."

"Aye, but she mightn't be too fond a lavin' 'er friends."

"Go ahead anyway," said Molly, "an' see how yis get on."

As they were about to leave, a loud knock on the door startled them. Tom opened it to find the little slim figure of Jock Sullivan on the doorstep.

Well wrapped up in a tweed overcoat, scarf and cap, he smiled and looked relieved that it was Tom who answered his knock.

"Good Morra, Tom; what way a ye?"

"I'm not too bad, Dinny, how's yerself?"

"Oh, couldn't be better, Tom ... I come over te have a word with ye."

"Fair enough ...will ye come in?"

"Oh damit no, not atall ... this bit a business is between ourselves, out here'll do the finest."

"I'll tell 'em inside." He whispered to Molly that it was Jock Sullivan and he wouldn't be long and went out again.

Molly had never heard of Jock Sullivan but Tom knew him all his life. He was a tough, hardy devil that spent all his early years riding horses. He followed the hunt and won hundreds of Point-to-Point races. He was a reckless character in a race, feared by all the other riders and even the horses. The terrible fall he got one day in Rochestown would have killed any other man. After breaking nearly every bone in his body, he survived and recovered with only a limp to show for it.

But that finished him riding. He took over the running of the home farm from his elderly father, settled down and got a woman.

But he always kept plenty horses about the place, and people were often amazed in the spring of the year to see him following four horses under a big wide harrow at all hours tilling the big fields that made up his three hundred acres. How he done all the walking was a mystery with his patched-up body.

"We'll go over here out o' the cowld," said Tom. The frosty fog was descending and the cow house door was open.

"Well now, Tom, I'll state me case ... what brings me here is te see would ye be wantin' a job? ... the spring is comin' an' I'll have te get someone."

"What kind of a job, Dinny?"

'Damit man, sure ye know the job that I'd have ... tillin' the bleddy land a course."

"Ye mane, follyin' horses?"

"No," a smile lit up his wrinkled face, "the horses are a thing of the past ... I'm goin' with the times ... I have a new tractor ordered an' I want a good man te drive it ... I heard you're a great man at the wheel."

"What's the money like?"

"Sure damit man I'll pay the standard wages … thirty-six shillin's a week …five an a half days … an yer dinner an' supper."

"That's a long way below what I have now, Dinny."

"But sure ye'd be at home man, with yer wife an children … an' t'would save ye havin' te keep two houses an' all that bleddy peddlin'."

"I'll have te think about it."

"Damit man, sure there's nothin' te think about … you want a good job an' I want a good man … sure t'would suit the two of us down te the ground."

"Could ye wait a minute till I tell herself about it?"

"Not a bother, Tom …you go ahead an' I'll wait here."

He beckoned Molly down to the little parlour, closed the door and quietly told her. She stood speechless in front of him while she let it sink in and tried to focus her thoughts.

"Oh, Tom, I don't know what te say … sure tis you'll have te have the last word on it."

"Ah no …the two of us."

"T'will be your job, Tom, an' I won't tell ye one way or t'other … can't ye tell 'em you'll let 'em know to-morrow; he surely can wait wan day."

"Will you come out an' ask 'em?"

She went out with him. Sullivan was sitting on the old milking stool. He stood up and put out his hand to greet Molly.

"Pleased te meet ye, Missis … What way a' ye?

"Grand thanks."

"Ye have a big family?"

"We have four boys and wan girl."

"Oh God bless 'em all … that takes some feedin'."

"Have ye children yerself?"

"Oh be God, I have surely … Denis is ninteen an' Maura is eighteen an' the two o' them are in collage in Dublin … Poor Nancy can't go anywhere … she's seventeen, but sure the poor crater is not the whole shillin'."

"Oh, I'm sorry te hear that," said Molly, "but sure I suppose 'tis the will o' God."

"'Tis hard te know, Missis … t'was late when we started … maybe that's the rason … what d'ye think o' the bit a business meself an' Tom are doin'?"

Molly looked at Tom. He gave her a slight nod to go ahead and have her say.

"Well, Mr Sullivan, t'would be a big change for us all an' we'd have te think an' talk about it before we could make up our minds … would tomorra be alright te tell ye?"

He gazed at the ground, lifted his cap and scratched his bald head in thought.

"We'll let ye know for certain one way or t'other tomorra." Molly repeated.

He straightened up.

"I have another couple o' fellas I could ask … but sure I can wait 'till tomorra … you're the man I want, Tom."

"We'll let ye know tomorra," said Tom.

"That'll do … I'll head off so … God be with yis."

They watched him limp down the grassy lane to his small Ford van. Tom shouted after him.

"Ye can lave the gate open … I'll be goin' out there in a minute."

He waved back, got into the van and drove away.

"We better go or t'will be dark."

"I'll send out the chaps."

Johnny Moran spotted them from the kitchen window as they entered the yard and quickly joined them.

"Christ God, I thought yis were't comin' atall … I was nearly givin' up on yis."

"I got delayed," said Tom, "Jock Sullivan came up just as we were comin' out the door."

"Oh Jasus! The Jock! Was that who owned the van at the gate? … I was wonderin'."

"That was him … He's houldin' out well."

"D'ye know what I'm goin' te tell ye, Tom … tha's a hardy hoor, that fella."

"He is," said Tom, thinking about the growing darkness, "Here Johnny, I better pay ye."

He handed him the ten pound note.

"Oh, Christ God, a bit a luck, hould on there."

He went inside and came out looking at the coins in his hand.

"Now, Tom, a half crown for you an' a shillin' each for the chaps."

'Begor, thanks Johnny, we didn't expect that."

"They'll be money when we're dead, Tom … good luck with 'er now."

Tom told Paschal to go over the lane in front and Robbie to stand at the other side. Timmy and himself would go behind. Johnny untied the heifer and she went quietly over the lane, up into the yard and into the little cow house.

Tom and Molly didn't discuss the job offer until Granny and the children were gone to bed. It was nearing their bedtime too. They sat at each side of the fire and they knew that it was decision time.

"What d'ye think, Tom?"

"Begob, I dunno … what d'you think?"

'Sure, Tom, I don't know the first thing about that Sullivan man."

"I know 'em all me life."

"An' would he be alright te work for?"

"I suppose he would … he's a hard go'er himself … but sure ye'd have te work where ever ye'd be."

"But would he kill ye workin', Tom?"

"Ah, ye wouldn't be too bad drivin a new tractor … no, the job'd do alright; 'tis the money I'd be thinkin' about … thirty-six shillin's is a long way from what I have."

Molly stared into the fire in deep thought, then quickly switched her focus back to him.

"But, Tom, it costs ye ten shillin's every week te work in Waterford … yi'd save that, an' ye wouldn't have all that hardship trudgin' up an' down."

"Oh, I know. Tha's true enough, but it still laves four shillin's of a difference."

She looked into his eyes with a concerned look.

"Tom! If ye took the job, de ye think ye might regret it later on … ye know, laven' Mr Quinlivan, an' Waterford, an' all?"

"No. Sure I know I have te get a job down here anyway ... we're done in Waterford."

"Well then, there's on'y wan thing te do."

"Wha's that?"

"Go te that man tomorra an' tell 'em y'ill take the job if he comes up the extra four shillin's."

"I wonder would he?"

"Well, ye won't know that 'till ye try 'em ... I bet ye he won't let ye go for the sake of four shillin's."

"Begob, ye might be right ... 'tis worth a chance."

"But Tom, before ye go; are ye sure now yer happy about it?"

He looked into her eyes and smiled.

"A course I'm happy about it ... sure won't I be here with you an' the lads every night."

'Oh, Tom, that would be the best thing of all."

She silently thanked the Blessed Mother as they both headed for the stairs.

*

Molly was first up. She had a little Sunday treat planned for them that she knew they would all enjoy, especially Tom. She lit the fire, hung the big flat pan on the crane, and soon the little kitchen was filled with the appetising smell of sizzling rashers, sausages and eggs. The whiff of that mouth-watering aroma reached upstairs and soon had them all at the table, ready for action. The children were delighted that porridge was off the menu for one day and their father was licking his lips too at the prospect of a real Irish breakfast. They sat in and when all the plates were clean, Robbie remarked that it was a pity that Sunday only came once a week.

"Now," said Tom, "the cow have to be milked."

"Oh ye," said Molly, "I better go out with ye so that I can milk 'er when yer gone."

It was another hard, frosty morning and the grassy yard felt solid under their feet. Molly opened the hen house door, the hens rushed out, leaving the clucking one resting snugly on her nest. She had claimed the laying box, preventing the others from using it. Still they managed to lay during the night and Timmy gathered four big eggs from under the roost and brought them in to be washed.

Tom got a wet cloth and cleaned the heifer's teats.

"Begob, she have a grand little bag a milk."

"God bless 'er," said Molly, I hope she won't mind ye bein' strange."

He sat on the stool, well in under her, with the galvanised bucket that Molly bought on Friday in Campile, held firmly between his knees. With his forehead tight to her flank, he tenderly fondled her teats and udder. He let the first milk wet his hands and without a murmur from the heifer, he began a steady rhythm. Molly and the children formed an audience and the children were fascinated with the song of the milk echoing against the bottom of the bucket. As the level of the milk gradually ascended and the froth formed, the song was gone but the heifer seemed to be even more contented. With the bag empty and the bucket almost half full, Tom stood up.

"She'll make a grand little cow."

"Oh, thanks be te God," said Molly, Johnny said that alright ... I'm glad now that I got 'er."

Tom and the boys then went over to Moran's and filled sacks of straw and hay. Johnny shouted at them that he would blow the horn at the gate on his way to Mass. When they got back they bedded and fed the heifer and went in to get ready for Mass.

He had to make a little detour on his way home from Mass to call to Jock Sullivan. Deep in thought as he peddled along, Tom was rehearsing in his mind the approach he would take and the words he would use in making his case. There could be only one outcome to his encounter with Jock ... either he coughed up the extra money or he would be staying in Waterford. Molly was fairly sure he would, but, knowing the man as *he* did, he wasn't so sure.

Sullivan's land covered the hill of Blakestown and the farmyard seemed to have been placed on the summit. A sprawling, untidy yard, surrounded by big sheds, lots of stables, and an array of abandoned farm machinery backed away from a large two-story dwelling house that looked out on the road. The big fields stretched out from all sides, giving an unrestricted view of the whole farm.

Tom was glad to see the van in the yard. As he rode in, a big black and white sheepdog greeted him with loud barking. He parked the bike against a stable wall and looked around. A capped head shot out over the half door of a stable. It was the Jock's.

"Oh, Tom! Good man! Over here."

He went over and into the stable where the Jock was washing a horse's leg that had a long gaping wound.

"Well, Tom, how are ye taday?"

"Oh, good, good, how's yerself?

"I'd be a damn sight better, Tom, if this hadn't te happen … this bleddy fool of a horse got 'emself caught in barbed wire … no where else'd do 'em te go."

"Ah sure, those things happen," said Tom , ye still have a lot a horses?"

"Too bleddy many … I'll have te get rid o' half o' 'em when I get the tractor … no use feedin' the feckers te do nothin'."

He put ointment on the cut and straightened up.

"Well, Tom, ye made up yer mind?"

"I did"

"Good man … when will ye be able te start?"

"Oh now, I didn't make up me mind te start."

Sullivan looked puzzled.

"Ye won't take the job?"

"I can't, Dinny … the money is the trouble."

"Sure, God damit man, I'm givin ye the standard wages … thirty-six shillin's a week."

"I know, Dinny, but it takes a lot te rear a big family."

The Jock turned away from Tom, walked a couple of steps with his face held in his hand as he contemplated. He turned back.

"Tom! I'll meet ye on it … thirty-eight."

Tom didn't have to think.

'No, Dinny, I couldn't."

Sullivan seemed agitated.

"Well, curse o' God on it, tell me what yer lookin' for then?"

'Well, Dinny, I'm under strict orders not to take any less than two pound a week."

"Strict orders! The missis is it?"

"Yeah,"

"Oh Jasus ... pettycoat government ... them bleddy women'd have the country broke if they had their way!"

Tom didn't reply.

The Jock inhaled a huge breath and blew it out in exasperation.

"Hould out yer hand." Tom did. "Y'ill have me in the bleddy poor-house ... two pound a week it is then ...let it be so."

He slapped Tom's hand to seal the deal.

"When will ye be able te start?"

"Would Monday week be all right?"

"Couldn't be better."

They shook hands, Tom mounted the bike and rode out of the yard.

Arriving home from Mass in the car with Johnny Moran, they noticed some of the hens had scratched their way down the grassy lane, out through the gate and were picking leisurely on the bog lane.

"Christ God, yis have hens!"

"We have," said Robbie.

"Don't run over 'em," said Timmy.

They ran out of the way.

Molly told Johnny about the hatching hen and her intention to set her.

"An' have ye eggs?"

"No, Johnny, we'll have te wait till we collect enough te put under 'er."

"Christ God, sure t'will be gone off of 'er be then ... Send over the chaps an' I'll give em a dozen ... there's eggs everywhere over there."

"Oh, Johnny, are ye sure ... I'll pay ye for 'em."

"Pay be God damned ... y'ill do no such a thing ...sure 'tis tryin' te get rid of 'em we are."

"Oh, thanks Johnny, I'll send over the chaps."

The children chattered their way up to the house. Molly was in deep thought. She had prayed to the Blessed Mother at Mass for Tom to have good news from his visit to Mister Sullivan. If everything worked out well with the job and he was happy with it, it would be a whole new life for all of them. It would save poor Tom the hardship of traipsing that long journey every week and being stuck on his own up there in that big old house. Her life with that old lady would be a lot more bearable too, knowing that Tom wouldn't be far away and having him home every night. She said another little prayer, before going inside, putting on the kettle, to have it boiling when Tom came home.

She couldn't concentrate for long on anything. Her mind was on Tom and the news he might bring home. She tried to keep busy with little jobs. The milk! It was still in the bucket on the floor covered with a towel. Placing it on the table and admiring it, she saw at least a gallon of lovely rich milk, and felt gratitude to God and to Johnny Moran too. She strained two pints into the big jug and the remainder into the enamel basin.

Granny wasn't taking any notice; she was in her chair by the fire fingering her beads and whispering her prayers. The children were all playing outside.

She carried the basin of milk into the parlour and laid it on a sheet of paper on the table. It would set overnight and then she would skim off the cream.. She could see that a week's milk from the little heifer would provide all the butter they needed and plenty buttermilk as well.

She was basking in the pleasure of a job well done when Granny shuffled past on her way to her room. She stopped and her eyes fixed on the basin of milk on the table.

'What's that doing there?"

"'Tis settin', Granny, I'm goin' te make butter."

"Take that away out of there … that's my good, polished table and you'll have the whole room messed up."

Molly was stunned.

"But sure Granny, where *will* I put it?"

"Put it out in the dairy where I always put it."

"But ye could put nothin' out there … that wasn't used for years; full of dirt and cobwebs."

"Can't you clean it … be something for you to be doing."

Molly was ready to explode. She took a deep breath, opened her mouth to release the fire but closed it again and held her patience. Tom would soon be home, maybe with good news, and she didn't want to cause an uproar that she might regret later. Taking the basin of milk back into the kitchen, she went upstairs.

Angry and upset, she went into the inside room and made the children's beds. While making her own bed she kept an eye out through the little gable window for a sighting of Tom. With no more to do she sat on the bed with a direct view out the window, keeping her eyes on the lower lane. She had a little chat with the Blessed Mother while she waited, and soon she saw the hunched figure of Tom peddling along; her heart skipped a beat.

Out in the yard, she told the children and they all raced down the lane to meet him. As he leaned the bike against the wall, Molly searched his face for a clue. A smirk and an emphatic wink told her the news was good.

Moving closer to him she whispered: "How did ye get on?"

"Oh, tip top ... ye were right ... he came up trumps."

"Two pound a week?"

"Yeah."

'Oh, Tom, that's great ... are ye happy with it now?"

"Course I am."

"When do he want ye?"

"Tomorra week."

"Well, thanks be te the Mother o' God."

"Tha's it now ... good bye Waterford."

"Well I hope te God it works out ... d'ye know, Tom, she attacked me again taday."

"Oh Ah ... about what?"

"She ate the face off me for puttin' the milk in the parlour."

"An' where were ye te put it."

"That's the thing, Tom ... she said te put it in the dairy."

"In there! ... t'would want some cleanin"

They went over to the little concrete room that was built as an extension to the house beside the kitchen door. With a small sash window and a slated roof, it hadn't been used for years. Tom forced the door open to be met by dirt, debris and mold.

"Maybe we could do somethin' with it."

"But sure Tom, ye have te go back te Waterford."

"Ah, I know, but I have a couple o' hours still."

"Well, come in first an' have yer tay."

"I will."

Sitting around the table, Molly announced the good news to the children. Their yelps of joy and excitement were so boisterous that Granny was becoming agitated and gesturing to their mother to stop them. But Molly was delighted for them and especially for Tom and herself.

While Tom, Molly and Paschal were scrubbing out the dairy, Robbie and Timmy went over to Moran's for the hatching eggs. In two hours of hard work, the dairy was bright and clean again, the eggs were under the hen and being hatched, and a new laying box was fixed in the other corner of the hen house. It was time for Tom to get ready for his last trip to Waterford.

*

It was Thursday and there was enough cream skimmed from five day's milk to make some butter. The little wooden churn hadn't been used for years and it had to be dismantled and scrubbed with boiling water. Mina and Kenny were excitedly watching her every move; it was all new to them. They could scarcely believe that the big bowl of cream was about to be turned into delicious butter that they would be putting on their bread and their potatoes.

There wasn't much space to work in the little dairy but Molly moved things to make room for the churn to be placed on the table, which was a comfortable height for the tiresome turning of the handle.

The bowl of thick, slightly sour cream came up half way in the churn. The paddles were nicely submerged and Molly turned the handle slowly to check the workings before replacing the cover firmly.

"How long will it be before we get butter?" asked Mina.

"About half an hour, if we keep turnin' an' don't stop."

"Can we turn it, Mammy?" asked Kenny.

"Yeah … when I get tired, yis can turn away."

The steady turning made a swishing rhythm as she turned evenly and the children watched with fascination.

"How will we know when the butter is after comin'?" asked Mina.

"The butter'll splash around in the buttermilk an' we'll know be the sound."

As her arms got tired, Molly changed from one to the other. She gave each of the children a turn, but they soon got tired and she had to continue herself. The splashing began and she could feel the weight of the butter on the paddles. Rising the cover slightly, she had a peep in; it was almost done. She turned for a while longer, backwards and forwards, squeezing all the buttermilk from the butter, then removed the cover, allowing the children to see inside and marvel at the miracle just performed by their mother.

Having emptied the buttermilk into a basin, she scooped the butter into the big bowl. She washed it with water and when completely free of buttermilk, added the salt until it tasted perfectly. With the wooden butter spades, she kneaded it, moulded it into blocks, adorning them with artistic designs on the top.

The buttermilk, thick and creamy, with flecks of butter, was stored in a big jug for drinks and bread-making. It was a heart-warming, labour of love for Molly, and she felt gratitude to the little heifer, and also to Johnny Moran.

DOWN MEMORY LANE

Molly loved the month of May. After weeks of looking forward to May Day, when it arrived, it didn't disappoint her. Out of bed early and dazzled by the shafts of morning sunlight shining through the gable window, she knew it marked the end of the harsh winter and she hoped it would signal the beginning of brighter and happier months ahead.

May Day that year fell on a Wednesday, and being a bank holiday, there was no school for the children. As Tom, herself and the family sat around the table for breakfast, the extra light and heat beaming through the little kitchen window promised a lovely day and Molly decided to act on a little idea that she had for a while. It only needed a good weather forecast to implement. She announced that, being such a lovely day, she would make a little journey. She would visit the place of her birth, the old family home in Haggard, and, taking the children with her, she would make a detour to the nearby seaside village of Duncannon. It was only three miles from Haggard, the children had never been there, and from her own childhood memories, she knew they would love its unique charm and its beautiful, safe, sandy beach.

"What d'ye think, Tom?"

"Oh, begob, with the fine day, an' the school shut an' all, sure 'tis a right day te go."

The children clapped and cheered. Tom milked the cow and headed off to work, Molly fed the hens and chickens and gathered the eggs, and the boys went out to catch and yoke the pony.

Having survived four months of her journey into the uncertain and the unknown, Molly felt a degree of relief rather than triumph. There were times when a quick and total evacuation was a distinct possibility. It was often a test of her endurance and strength of mind. There were many trials and tribulations, but so far, thank God, she refused to be defeated. The presence of Tom during times of friction between Granny and herself was her saving grace. She thanked the Mother of God for helping to get him home from Waterford; that was the key to her survival. The boys were doing well in school, but that long trek every day was tough on them. The summer holidays would be a welcome break.

Tom's new job had worked out fine, despite all her worrying that it might not. It was a good time of the year for him to begin. He quickly became absorbed in the spring's work; tilling and sowing, immersed in the clay of his native place. It seemed to enrich his soul, keeping him happy and contented. The new tractor helped too, and the boss, in his wisdom, leaving him alone to get on with it in his own way, was great for Tom. Molly knew that he was always a devoted worker and a land-lover, and if left alone the work would be done and done well.

She gave Granny her breakfast and made her snug and comfortable in her chair at the fireside. It was time to load up. She and Paschal sat on one side of the trap, while the four other children squeezed into the seat on the opposite side. They drove down the lane, through the railway gates and on to the main road.

Six miles through lush green countryside lay ahead of them, and Molly was intent on driving the pony at a leisurely pace and inhaling the beauty of it all. Fields of young barley and oats spread out like green carpets, cows and cattle lay peacefully in the fresh pasture, and sheep rested while their little lambs frolicked and played.

Molly explained the meaning of May Day to the children, and why it was marked and celebrated around the world. She had heard it all from her late father. He loved May Day and was always fascinated with its old superstitions, customs and traditions. She tried to remember some of the old beliefs and sayings about May Day.

A wet and a windy May filled the haggard with corn and hay.

A swarm of bees in May is worth a load of hay.

Mist in May, heat in June, makes harvest come right soon.

If you wash a blanket in May, you'll wash one of the family away.

Those who bathe in May, will soon be laid in the clay.

"Are they really true?" asked Paschal, "would these things happen?"

"Ah, not atall, there only oul sayin's an' folklore."

"An' why did they say them then?" asked Robbie.

"Ah sure, the oul people believed them, an' they handed 'em down to the younger people."

They passed by many farmhouses, most of which had a fresh coat of whitewash. Trees were now getting new green clothes after being naked all winter, and passing some old ruins of houses they could get the rich perfume of lilac, that continued to grow and flourish even in abandoned and deserted places. Molly loved lilac and inhaling the sweet aroma, thanked God for the gift of being alive and well, and able to enjoy that lovely little trip with her children.

The signpost on the 'Doctor's Cross' that said 'Duncannon (1 mile) was a welcome relief to the trap-full of people, and, if he could have read it, would have been a welcome sign for the little pony as well. The straight road that led from there through Mersheen, Blackhill, and into the village was all downhill, and soon the wide expanse of blue water came into view. Overlooking the village stood the 'Star of the Sea' church, beautifully positioned on its elevated site, elegant, ornate, and still as warm and appealing to Molly as the first time she saw it as a child.

As they rounded the corner at the Police Barracks and moved leisurely down the main street, the children were fascinated by the little white-washed, terraced houses that flanked each side. They all looked the same, except for the doors and windows that were painted an assortment of bright colours. Molly always loved that little street. It brought back happy memories of the many times her own mother took them to Duncannon. Thirty years had passed since, her mother was now gone, but those quaint little houses were still there, adding the same little old-world, fairytale effect to the village.

At the bottom of the street on one corner stood the old 'Hotel' and on the other corner the 'Strand Tavern' pub. In front the golden sand extended left and right for a mile through grassy dunes to the blue sea glistening in the sunshine. Over the gentle waves, the 'Hook Lighthouse' stood tall in the distance, as it did for almost eight hundred years, and equally ancient, the 'Military Fort' stood proudly on its ramparts, scanning the estuary, as it had done since the 1798 Irish Rebellion.

Molly explained some of the history behind those famous landmarks, and the older children were impressed, not only by the beauty and charm all around them, but also by their mother's knowledge of it all.

Having tied the pony to a ring in the wall at the entrance to the strand, they removed the cushions from the trap and went down to a quiet spot in the dunes where they sat in the sun admiring the whole exciting scene. They almost had it all to themselves, except for a few elderly people out for their morning walk. The tide was a long way out but appeared to be coming back in. The children took off their boots and headed out to meet it. Molly removed her shoes and stockings and joined them. There wasn't much wind but little waves still formed, breaking in white froth, to the delight of the children. To Molly's freshly-bared feet and legs, the water was like freezing ice, causing her shivers all over, but the young ones ran and splashed through it with excitement and exhilaration. It was pure magic and they made the most of it. Molly returned to her cushion, leaving the children to their fun and frolics for almost an hour.

It was time to go. Before loading up, they called to the 'Strand Stores', an old shop with fond memories for Molly. In the old days, her own mother never left Duncannon without a visit to the little shop and a bit of chat and banter with old Mr Joyce. Sadly they were both now history, but a young Mr Joyce was there now and has kept the shop exactly as it had always been. Lemonade and ice cream was relished by the children, and Molly got a nice little fruit cake to bring to Haggard, knowing that it would be a welcome treat with the tea.

The pony was well rested and showed new energy and enthusiasm as they trotted out of the village.

Some of the houses they passed on their way out had children playing and having fun on their day off from school.

"I'd love te live here like them," said Robbie.

"Me too," said Timmy, "we could swim every day."

Paschal was in reflective mood.

"Anywhere would be better than where we're livin' now."

Molly saw a sadness in his eyes and understood his feelings. He was now eleven and his mind was starting to focus on new places and things. The Bogside was alright for adults and people that liked a bit of peace and solitude, but it was no place for children to grow up in. She knew that Tom and his brothers and sisters were reared there and were none the worse for it, but those were different times. She really felt sorry for her children, especially the older ones. They saw nothing from one end of the week to the other, only a bog, a railway, an old hillside school every day, and a little country church on a Sunday.

She didn't know when she would get the chance to solve that problem, but solve it she would, whatever it took. Their stay in The Bogside would not be forever, and she suspected that with Granny slowly going down hill, it might be shorter than anyone thought. But then the thought crossed her mind that even if Granny was gone, Tom might want them to remain on in the little homestead. It was his birthplace and he loved it; she could understand that. But she had other ideas. The visit to Duncannon awakened possibilities and lit a spark in her that would not be quenched till she was out of The Bogside and relocated to somewhere with a bit of life in it. A place where they would be near things and not at the back of beyond, miles away from everything.

The children too, would see and do things and not be isolated as they were, looking out over an old bog, traipsing three miles to school every day, and nothing to interest or entertain them.

A new determination welled up inside her and she pledged to herself that their exile in The Bogside would be short-lived, whatever it took to make it happen.

As the pony and trap left the main road and turned into Haggard lane, memories began flooding back to Molly and intensified as her old childhood home came into view.

A County Council labourer's cottage, one of hundreds dotted throughout County Wexford, it was dry, cosy and warm, with two rooms on the ground floor and two upstairs, outhouses for hens and pigs, and a half acre of land to the rear.

As the pony and trap-load of unexpected visitors stopped at the gate, Molly's brother, Nicky, rose from his kneeling position beside his motorbike in the middle of the yard. Holding up his two oil-soaked hands in welcome, he went towards them to open the gate.

"Jasus, Molly, wha' way a ye? Yer the last wan I expected te see … An' the children … Christ, 'tis great te see yis."

"Ah, sure we're grand, Nicky … how a' you an' the family?"

"Oh, not a bit a fear of us, Girl … aint it a fright now, the wan day ye came, Minnie is gone home te see 'er father an' I'm stuck in this oul bike."

"Don't mind us atall … carry on what yer doin' … where are the children?"

"The chaps are out in the field playin' football and Jenny is gone with 'er mother."

That message reached the ears of Paschal, Robbie and Timmy. They ran out to join their cousins, Larry, who was twelve and Danny, who was ten. Soon, a proper football match was in progress, with the added treat of real goalposts.

"Is the motorbike broke down?"

"Oh, 'tis not, but when I got the day off work, I done a bit of a service on it; changed the oil and cleaned the plugs an' things … I'll just put in this plug now an' I'll be finished."

"It must have been tough ridin' that te Ross all the winter?"

"Oh, Jasus, Molly, t'would take yer feckin' life … some frosty morn's I'd have icicles hangin' out o' me nose."

"Ye should try an' get a little motorcar."

"A motorcar! Are ye out o' yer head? I'd want te win the sweep or somethin'."

He finished with the motorbike, washed his hands in parofin oil and ushered Molly into her old familiar kitchen.

"Sit down there an' I'll make the tay."

"No, I'll make it; you sit down."

She was glad to see that very little had changed in the house since their father and mother died and Nicky, Minnie and the children moved in. Looking around the kitchen, seeing again the old pictures and mementoes of her childhood, gave her a nostalgic feeling of going back in time. A cloud of sadness hovered in her mind at the absence of her parents, and the memories of the years of life they all shared that little kitchen.

When the tea was ready, Nicky shouted to the footballers to come in and they all enjoyed a welcome meal, especially Molly's 'Duncannon' fruit cake.

When the children returned to the football field, Nicky and Molly chatted about the old days and how life was for both of them. She was the eldest of the family, and he was next, ahead of two other boys, Paddy and Jimmy, now in London with Aggie, and the two other girls Nellie and Nan who were married in Ireland. She always thought of him as the wisest one, and if she ever had a problem she would ask for his advice, which he was always happy to give. They discussed life in The Bogside.

"I'll tell ye what ye should do, Molly … apply to the County Council for a cottage … they're buyin' one-acre sites from the farmers all over the place now, an' buildin' cottages for the people on the housin' list."

"How could we get on the housin' list, Nicky?"

"No bother … get the doctor to condemn the house you're livin' in, an' ye'll get on the list"

" Oh yeah; I'd say that could be done alright … sure any doctor would see that our little shack wasn't fit for a family of five."

"There ye go … ye could be livin' in a brand new house by this time next year."

"Oh, Nicky, thanks for tellin' me all that … I'll get goin' on it straight away."

"I know ye will, an ye won't stop till ye get it … you never took no for an answer, Molly."

"Ah, I don't know about that … we'll have te go soon, Nicky … I'm delighted I came, an' that ye were here."

They loaded into the trap. Nicky led the pony out to the road. He turned suddenly.

"Oh, Jasus, lads … I nearly forgot … d'yis want a pup?"

The children looked at each other and at their mother.

"What kind of a pup, Nicky?" asked Molly.

The bitch had four … two are gone te good homes, and there's two left … hould on there 'till I show yis."

He went around the back of the house and came back with two lovely terrier puppies with black and white spots.

"Awe, there beautiful," said Molly.

"Yis can take whichever wan yis like."

When Molly saw the excitement in the eyes of the children, she couldn't refuse the kind offer.

"But there's no room in the trap … where will we put em?"

"We'll carry 'em on our lap," said Robbie.

"Yeah we will," they all joined in.

They decided which one they liked best, Nicky put him in a shopping bag, the boys agreed to take him in turns on their laps.

As the pony quickened into a trot and left the old homestead behind, a happy family smiled, laughed and chatted the six miles that would end at the railway gates, and take them home after an enjoyable day trip, back again to the dull and dreary life on The Bogside.

A Trip to the Fair

It was the third week of a lovely month of May weather. Molly was glad of the chance to be outside of the house as much as she could. Granny was a permanent fixture at the fireside and the words that they exchanged were few and far between. Molly could see that she was slowly fading, eating less, getting smaller and sleeping a lot. But she still had the angry fire that could ignite at any moment, and to avoid the flying sparks, Molly kept her distance as much as she could.

The sun was beaming down from a clear blue sky as she stood outside the door and surveyed the little yard that had been transformed over the five months since that cold January day when they arrived in the big van and embarked on a mission of trials and tribulations that at times tested her patience and endurance, and challenged her to find resources that she didn't even know she had.

It had taken her a week of scratching and scraping to finally get rid of the grassy sods that covered the yard. The whitewashing of the walls gave her pains in her limbs from the bending and brushing, and aches in her heart from the mean comments of Granny that she had no authority to do it.

But it was worth it; that little yard had now come alive. The little heifer was a gift from God, giving them lots of milk, butter and buttermilk. The hens were laying lovely big brown eggs. The chickens, having left their mother, were growing into nice poultry. The pony, donkey and heifer were blooming in the lush May pasture of the little field, and the terrier puppy had grown big enough to chase them away if they came near the yard and invaded his territory.

Molly gazed at the little piggery, empty and derelict, and scratching her head, decided it was time to restore it and put it to use. Rolling up her sleeves, she made a start. In a few hours of determined action the little eyesore was transformed. With all the old dried slurry scraped from the floor, the walls whitewashed, and the concrete feeding trough scrubbed clean, she stood back and admired it. It was now ready for use, no longer an grey and desolate, and even blended in well with the other outhouses. The next thing was to get a couple of tenants for it; Molly had an idea for that too.

The village of Campile was one long wide street. It had three pubs, two shops, and a big Co-Op store. About three hundred people lived in the street and around the edges. On the third Wednesday of every month its population trebled as the farmers from a wide area swarmed in for the monthly fair, and occupied the main street with a mixed variety of cattle, sheep and pigs.

Molly had left home early, just as the boys were leaving for school. When she had Granny fixed up and snug by the fireside, she yoked the pony and set off for Campile. Mina and Kenny were excited but didn't really know what to expect. Approaching the village, she wondered where she might tie the pony. Both sides of the street were crowded with clusters of cattle, pens of sheep, horses and carts, some loaded with pigs, others with calves. She drove into Hart's yard and found a vacant spot.

With a child at each side she made her way up the street, through the moving mass of noisy chatter, intent on taking in the whole scene, before focussing her mind on the real purpose of her visit.

Halfway up, 'Cheap John' a street trader who was part of the furniture at fairs all over the country was shouting and singing the praises of his ware, He had everything from a needle to an anchor, and the crowd, three-deep around him were captivated by his demonstrations and were hypnotised into making purchases that they didn't really need.

Molly was fascinated by the 'Tanglers'. They were the deal-makers between the farmers and the Cattle Buyers. Little men with weather-beaten faces; they had the 'gift of the gab' and persistence to match. Watching them operate so cunningly, Molly figured that they earned whatever little they got, and the fairs would be lost without them.

The three pubs seemed to be overflowing. Buyers and sellers were celebrating and some were drinking in little groups outside the doors.

Molly and the children had almost reached the top of the street. That was the area for the pigs. Litters of lovely white bonhams were sleeping in deep beds of straw in cart-creels. The horses and ponies tied to the wall were half asleep too. A shout from behind startled her.

"Molly!"

She turned. At first she didn't recognise the speaker. A tall man in a striped shirt and tweed jacket was smiling warmly in her direction. It couldn't be … it was … Tom's younger brother Tim !! She shouldn't have been so surprised. Sure she knew that the little farm where he lived with his Aunt was near Campile.

"Tim! I didn't know ye … I'm sorry, I never expected te see ye here … are ye sellin' or buyin'?"

"Oh, begor, I'm tryin' te sell these few pigs."

He showed them the sleeping piglets and the children put their hands in through the creels and stroked their backs.

"I suppose ye want te sell the whole litter together, Tim?"

"Begor, I would if I could get a customer."

"I was lookin' te buy two pigs te put in the little piggery, but I suppose t'would be hard te get someone te sell two from a litter."

"Begor, ye can pick the best two o' them, if ye like … I'd sell 'em anyway atall."

"How much are ye lookin' for 'em?"

"I was hopin' te get twelve shillins a piece, but sure, Molly, I can't be hard on you … pick the two best an' I'll give 'em te ye for ten bob apiece … a pound for the two."

"Oh, God, Tim, I will. … that's great … I'm lucky I met ye now."

"How are ye goin' te get 'em home?"

"I have the pony an' trap in Hart's yard, an' I have a big jute bag te put 'em in."

"Oh, fair enough … we'll go down te Kenny's first for a little drink an' a chat. God, I haven't seen ye for years."

Molly paid Tim for the pigs and wanted to treat him to a drink for giving her such a good deal.

"Not atall … this is on me … 'tis great te meet yis."

Molly always liked Tim. He was different than all the others; full of fun and mischief, light-hearted and easy-going. He was adored by his aunt Bridgie, who treated him like a child and left him short of nothing. He grew up to be a generous and kind man, popular with everyone, especially the women.

After a wide-ranging chat that lasted nearly an hour, they returned to the street and Tim drove his white pony and his load of pigs to Hart's yard. He put the best two into the bag, tied it and transferred it to the floor of Molly's trap. They were big strong piglets and as they grunted their protests, Mina and Kenny kept their feet up under them on the seat. Tim fumbled in his pockets and located two sixpence pieces and despite their mother's protest gave them to the children.

"I hope ye sell the rest of em now, Tim"

"I will a course, plenty buyers up there still."

As he said goodbye and manoeuvred his white pony and cart back up through the congested street, Molly and the children waved goodbye, and with two pigs in a bag, grunting their protests, they headed off in the other direction.

SAD FRIDAY

It was Friday, the first day of June. Molly had been to Campile in the forenoon for the week's shopping. A wild banging on the door, that sounded like thunder, startled her, and alerted Granny's attention too. It was early afternoon and the noise vibrated around the little quiet kitchen. Alarmed, the two women looked at each other and then heard loud shouting above the banging.

"See who it is," demanded Granny of a stunned Molly.

She gingerly opened the door to find a distraught Johnny Moran with his mouth open and his eyes ready to pop out.

"Me Mother! Me Mother! She's dyin'! … She's dyin'! … will ye come quick, Missis? An stay wud 'er 'til I go for the priest an' the doctor!"

"Oh, Johnny, what happened?"

"She was just goin' across the kitchen an' fell straight down."

Molly grabbed her coat off the back of the door and shouted in to Granny.

"I must go wud Johnny, his mother is after fallin' … I'll have te leave the children with you."

They rushed over the lane and in to the house.

Lizzie Moran hadn't stirred from where Johnny left her on the floor of the parlour with a pillow under her head and a blanket over her. Molly stroked her wrinkled forehead and held her limp hand. She was in a deep sleep and breathing heavily.

"She's unconscious, Johnny."

"Oh, Jasus , Missis; is she? What'll we do?"

He showed her the spare bedroom off the parlour with a double bed in it.

"Will we try an' lift 'er in?"

"Oh no Johnny. No. We won't disturb 'er."

"Christ God I'll go for the priest an' the doctor ... will ye be alright 'till I come back?"

The thought of being alone with a dying woman terrified Molly, but she couldn't let Johnny down.

"Go on Johnny ... quick as ye can ... I'll mind 'er."

The fear and anxiety in his eyes softened to a look of affection and gratitude as he ran out, jumped into the motorcar and revved out of the yard.

Molly couldn't do anything to help the old woman. The breathing was deep and course and becoming strained and erratic. She prayed fervently to the Blessed Mother to keep her alive until the priest and doctor came. Every minute felt like an hour. She held the bony hands and kept whispering softly, although she knew her words were not being heard. Gently massaging her face and stroking her silver hair back from her forehead, she noticed the flushed red colour fading to a cold grey.

"Oh, Jesus, Mary and Joseph; please don't take her 'till Johnny comes back."

The big clock in the hall chimed three o'clock, startling Molly, as it loudly invaded the gloomy silence. But it told her that Johnny was half an hour gone and she hoped he would be back in the next half an hour.

There was no response from Lizzie to her gentle stroking and soft whispering. The breathing was getting even harsher, changing at times to intermittent snoring. But she didn't seem to be in any pain or discomfort. It was just a deep sleep without the slightest movement of any limb. Molly feared the worst, but prayed that it would not come yet.

The doctor's motorcar drove into the yard followed by Johnny's. While he examined the patient, Molly and Johnny waited in the kitchen.

"What about the priest, Johnny?"

"He wasn't there ... I left word wid the housekeeper ... She said he wouldn't be long and he'd come straight away."

The doctor called them down.

'She's suffered a bad stroke ... Can we get her into a bed?"

"Oh yeah, in here," said Johnny.

They removed the blankets, carried her in gently, placed her in the centre of the bed and replaced the blankets.

"Is she bet, Doctor?" Johnny had a tremor in his voice.

"She may last a few hours."

Johnny's gaze dropped to the floor. Molly placed her hand on his shoulder.

Not long after the doctor had left, the priest's motorcar entered the yard. Johnny went out to bring him in.

"This is our new neighbour, Father, Missis Coonan. They shook hands.

"You need a good neighbour to-day, Johnny."

"I sure do, Father … this woman is the best."

He told the priest what the doctor had said.

"I know, Johnny, we met at the railway gates and he told me."

Johnny shook his head and struggled to hold back the tears. They lit a blessed candle, got the holy water, and Father Donovan anointed Lizzie. She never blinked but her breathing became hoarse and laboured.

"Not a good sign," said the priest., we'll say the rosary."

They knelt down and began. Molly and Johnny were at opposite sides of the bed and held her hands as the priest led the rosary.

The breathing became more of a struggle, her mouth opened and the pauses between breaths became longer. The priest changed from the beads to the book and began to read the prayers for the dying. Tears flowed down Johnny's cheeks as his mother's long gasps turned into 'death rattles'. Molly too, could no longer hold back the tears. Between each long noisy breath, they held their own breaths, willing her to struggle on. The pauses became longer but still she managed to find more. Father Donovan kept reading. Johnny's anguish intensified, and Molly felt blessed to be so intimately involved in the passing of such a brave spirit. A long rattling gasp, that vibrated her whole face, seemed to have come from the depths of her being and as the priest paused in his reading and they waited for another, there was only silence, and tears, and resignation to God's will.

The priest laid his hand on the now still forehead.

"She's happy now. God took her on the day that she would have wished."

He saw the puzzlement in their eyes.

"The 'First Friday'! When she was able she never missed mass and the sacraments every 'First Friday'"

"Oh, 'tis true alright, Father, said Johnny, his face bathed in tears, she was a great 'First Friday' woman ... God tha's a miracle."

"I'll have to head back now, said the priest, I'll announce it at the prayers in church this evening. I'll call later to-night to say the rosary and we'll make the arrangements for the funeral."

"Oh, tha's good, Father, thanks very much."

As Johnny was seeing the priest to his car, Markie Kehoe's wife was crossing the yard towards the house. He joined her on the doorstep.

"How is she now, Johnny?" He had told her when she opened the railway gates for him on his way out. His mouth pursed and his chin trembled. Words wouldn't come. She got the message.

"She's gone to God?"

With tears streaming down his face and dropping off his chin he just nodded his head in agreement.

While Johnny was gone to the undertakers in Ballycullane, and to collect the woman that did the laying out, Molly and Betty prepared the house for the wake. There wasn't much to be done because Lizzie Moran's house was always clean and tidy. They stopped the clocks, closed the window blinds, and got every chair they could find ready for the wake room.

Molly knew the time her boys would be passing Moran's on their way home from school. From the doorstep she could see if they were coming down the field to the stile leading on to the lane. After a couple of looks, she saw them strolling leisurely down along the pathway. She met them at the gate but didn't tell them the full truth. It might be too much of a shock for Granny to be told by the children.

"Poor Missis Moran is very sick ... I have to stay here now an' yous go over an' stay with Granny until Daddy comes home."

"When will you be home, Mammy," asked Robbie.

"I don't know, Pet; as soon as I can."

With sadness in their eyes, they walked slowly over the lane.

When Johnny arrived back, he had a big woman sitting up beside him in the motorcar, and the back seat was full of cardboard boxes. Molly never met Lil Quinn, but had heard of her. Tom often mentioned her and said that after the priest, the doctor and the teacher, she was the next most important person in the parish, because as a midwife, she brought the people into the world, and as a layer-outer, she sent them out of it.

Johnny carried in the bags and introduced Molly to her. She already knew Betty Kehoe. Her hand clasp startled Molly with its strength and grip. Six feet tall, she looked about fifty, with sharp eyes, high cheek bones and strong limbs. She towered over the others, and to Molly, she appeared to be a no-nonsense, determined woman, that knew her job and expected her assistants to be likewise.

Johnny carried in the boxes and placed them on the table. One was from the undertaker and full of everything Lil needed. The others were packed with food and drink for the wake. He extracted a bottle of Powers whiskey and got a glass from the press. He filled it to the brim and gave it to Lil. She sat at the table and seemed to relish it.

"Will yis have a drop?" He asked the two women.

Both said no.

"Yis'll have te have somethin'!"

"Maybe a drop of wine," said Betty, if ye have it."

"Christ God, I have."

"I'll have a drop a lemonade," said Molly.

"Oh God, Missis, a tee-totaller, the same as me poor mother down in the bed ... never touched a drop in her life."

"Have a sup yourself, Johnny," said Lil, "you could do with a drop now ... T'would crown you."

"Christ God, I won't, I'll have a sup after."

Lil began her work.

"D'ye want anythin'?" asked Johnny.

"A basin of steaming hot water and a couple of towels … And these women'll give me a hand."

It was the first time that Molly had been present at a laying-out. Lil seemed to be an expert. They lifted the still limp body in a sheet on to the floor and made the bed with clean sheets and pillow-cases.

"She died in her clothes," said Lil, we'll have to strip her."

Anything that was tight-fitting was cut off with a scissors.

Naked, they turned her over. Cotton wool sealed all outlets. The white habit, with embroidered breastplate, long sleeves with flared cuffs, and tying ribbons fitted her nicely. They lifted her back on to the bed. Lil shaped her gaunt face and toothless mouth with balls of cotton wool. She placed a prayer book under her chin and tied it around her head with a string. They raised her head and shoulders with high pillows and clasped her hands over the quilt, with her rosary beads entwined around her fingers.

Lil released the string on her head and removed the prayer book. The mouth remained closed, and with an extra few little delicate touches, she even arranged a little smile. They stuffed the clothes in a bag and tidied up.

Pictures were taken down and the chairs were arranged around the walls. The bedside table was draped with a white cloth. Two candles were lit in glass candlesticks and a bowel of holy water with a feather, was placed on the table.

Standing back to admire the work, Molly now knew what an expert Lil was. The old woman looked beautiful. She had none of the wrinkles, lines, or the ravishes of the years; she looked peaceful and tranquil. It was a work of art.

They opened the door and Lil called Johnny. Gingerly, with his head bowed and his hands nervously clasped in front of him, he entered the room. The glow of the candles appeared to transform his mother's grey complexion to a warm cream. The smile that Lil managed to create gave a reassurance of peace, contentment and happiness. With his face flushed and tearful, he kissed his mother's forehead and sprinkled her all over with holy water. Lil moved close to his ear.

"Are you happy now with what we done?'

He just nodded, sobbed, and went back to the kitchen. When Lil had lowered another large glass of whiskey, he loaded her into the motorcar and drove her home.

Later in the evening the house was full. They heard it from Father Donovan at the 'First Friday' prayers. They came into the room shyly, knelt by the bed, said a silent prayer and sprinkled the corpse with holy water. Older people sat on the chairs around by the walls. Voices were kept low, but they all talked the praises of Missis Moran, the nice woman she was, and how she didn't look half her age. Johnny's name was mentioned by everybody. Left alone now to fend for himself, they speculated on how he would manage, Some said he would be grand; others were not so sure. The general consensus was that there was only one thing he should do: "Get a woman."

Molly got the chance to go over to her house when the crowds started to come. Tom had heard the news on his way home from work. The children were after their supper and Granny was in her chair, having just finished saying the rosary for Lizzie Moran.

"She's a year older than me."

"Te see the job Lil Quinn done on 'er, ye'd never think she was eighty-one," said Molly.

"She always looked fresh. The only trouble she had was the back … she was a fine woman only for that."

"God, said Molly, "didn't she go out of the world quick."

"Ah! Sure didn't she get a good while out of it? Time for her to go."

Molly had no answer to that.

After fixing up Granny, the children and the house for the night, Tom and herself went back over to the wake. Johnny introduced them to his uncle, Martin, who had cycled ten miles from Saint Kearns. A low, stout man, with a wide, rugged face and a broad rimmed hat, Molly thought he didn't look a bit like Lizzie, but Tom had met him before and knew all about him.

Johnny poured a whiskey for Tom and a lemonade for Molly, and asked Tom would he mind digging the grave with Martin?

"I will a course," said Tom.

The priest arrived and there was a hushed silence. He led the rosary and they all prayed with a clear united response.

When the priest left, it was time for some to head home. Others, that were staying the night wandered outside for a smoke or a breath of fresh air. The atmosphere lightened and jokes and laughter began. It was a bright moonlit night, and older men, having examined the sky, said it would be a fine weekend for the funeral.

It was well after mid-night when Tom and Molly decided to go home.

"There's enough stayin' for the night," said Johnny, as he saw them out and thanked Molly.

:Christ God, on'y for ye, wha' wud I do?"

"Ah, 'tis nothin' Johnny, sure anyone would help at a time like that."

"I know, but thanks all the same."

On the way over the lane, Tom told Molly the full story about Martin. He wasn't really Johnny's uncle. Lizzie's sister had him when she was young, and they reared him and always pretended that he was their young brother. They spoiled him so much, that he was never any good to work, and only for they left him in the old house, he'd be homeless.

"What age would he be now?" asked Molly.

"He'd be in his mid-sixties, but he's lucky to be alive atall."

"Why?"

"Back in 1920 he was in the IRA and they were gettin' bombs ready in an oul house in Saint Kearns to blow up an Army Barracks when the whole lot exploded. Five were killed and nine were badly injured, but Martin was lucky. He had just left the others to go home for somethin', and heard the bang.

'Oh my God!' said Molly, holding her hands to her mouth, "It wasn't his time te go ... but it still must have affected him."

"Oh, it left a mark alright ... he's a odd kind of fella ... but a great character all the same."

As they passed through the little dark kitchen and up the stairs, Molly sighed, and reflected on what can happen in one afternoon.

Driving the diggers to the graveyard, Johnny was rubbing the sleep from his eyes and yawning after having being up all night.

"You better get a sleep tonight," said Martin, "I'll stand in for ye."

"Christ God, sure you'll be worse then, after two nights up,"

"That wouldn't bother me ... I could do ad'out sleep for a week."

Passing through Ballycullane, he stopped at Power's pub.

"Wud yis care te come in?"

"Ah, no," said Tom, we better go an' do the job now."

Johnny went in and returned with a cardboard box. Martin had a peep and saw two 'Baby Power' whiskeys and six bottles of stout.

"We won't be dry anyway,"

Tom had a look.

"That'll go well with the sandwiches," said Tom.

Molly had made a big parcel of sandwiches for them.

The little cemetery at Kinnagh was the resting place of all the Moran's. Ancient and isolated, it dated back nearly three hundred years. Enclosed by a mellow stone wall and surrounded by tall beech trees, it had been full for many years, and only people with existing family graves could be buried there.

Martin led them to the Moran plot in the far corner beneath a canopy of overhanging trees that were fully clothed in their summer foliage. It was behind the ruins of a little old chapel that had collapsed over the years, leaving only heaps of stones and one ivy-clad gable that still stood, defiantly refusing to surrender and fall.

It was a double plot and Martin knew that Lizzie had to go on the right; her husband, Mike, had rested for the past ten years on the left.

They gathered up the fine gravel that covered the grave and having marked out the size with pegs, started digging.

"I'll have te go … will yis be alright now?" said Johnny … I'll be back for yis in the evenin."

"Course we will," said Tom, "sure we have everythin' we want."

They had two good, sharp shovels, a pickaxe and a crowbar. The sun was warm and the coats had to be thrown to one side. The digging was easy at first and they were down three feet in a short time. But as they met more hardness and the elbow room was scarce, their progress slowed. Tom would use the pickaxe and Martin would climb down and throw up the loose clay. When they stopped to rest, the peace and quiet was noticeable, and only the gentle breeze rustling the leaves of the trees broke the eerie silence.

"One good thing anyway," said Martin, "there's no rocks here."

"We don't want any," said Tom.

At about five feet deep, they stripped the side of a coffin.

"We're lucky," said Martin, "that's the boss now ... we barely missed 'em ... if we had te hit 'em with the pick; we'd have some mess."

"She'll be back close to 'em again," said Tom.

"Couldn't be any closer ... they can continue where they left off."

Tom smiled, but couldn't think of anything to follow that.

They rested, drank and ate. Tom wandered around, reading the old headstones. Some dated back to 1750, but others must have been there even longer because they were so worn and tilted with the years, they couldn't be read. Some big swanky graves had Celtic Crosses that stood tall and erect. He concluded that they were probably the 'Landed Gentry' – class distinction, he thought, even in the graveyard.

When they reached a depth of almost of seven feet, they decided it was deep enough. They trimmed the sides into the coffin shape and levelled the floor. They then tidied the big heap of clay and cleared the area above the mouth of the grave. The sun had disappeared behind some dark clouds, and in the chilliness, they put on their coats and waited for Johnny.

Father Donovan prayed for Lizzie Moran at mass on Sunday and announced that her funeral would be leaving the house at half past two for Kinnagh Cemetery. Requiem Mass for the repose of her soul would be on Monday at half past ten.

The old pot-holed lane hadn't seen so much traffic since the funeral of Mike Moran ten years ago. The house was full and some of the mourners had to move out to the yard to let others in for a last look. The priest said the prayers and the undertaker, Patrick Power, was waiting outside with the big black hearse and coffin backed up near the door.

The yard was filled with the crowd spilling out from the house. Tom carried in the coffin with the undertaker and stayed to help him in the closed wake room. Before the cover went on, Johnny was called down. Sobbing with anguish, he knelt beside the coffin on the floor. Clasping her hands and stroking her face, he kissed her tenderly on the forehead. Reluctant to let go, the undertaker helped him up. Knowing that it was his last sight of her, he slowly backed out the door, his tearful eyes fixed on the coffin filled with the love of his life and waited till it was closed and he would see her no more.

THINKING TIME

It was the first day of July and the hot sun beamed down from a clear blue sky. Molly felt it was the warmest day of the summer so far, as she walked over the lane to Moran's. In the month since Lizzie died, she managed to find a little time every day to go over and do a bit of housework for Johnny. She knew he appreciated it because he always made sure to have some little token for her as she left. Some days it would be a few big blue duck eggs or a couple of nice round turnips, and sometimes he would have dug a bucket of new spuds or filled a sack of kindling from under the saw bench.

She didn't expect anything, and told him so, but she gladly accepted, because she knew it came from the heart, and it made him feel better.

Martin had stayed with him for two weeks. That helped to ease the loneliness and the pain of losing his mother so suddenly. Johnny and Martin got on well, but Martin had his own house and he couldn't leave it locked up any longer. Johnny understood, was very thankful for what he did, and tying his bike on the back of the motorcar, he drove him home to Saint Kearns.

Molly could see that Johnny was still grieving; his good humour and cheerfulness had deserted him. When he spoke, she could hear the anguish in his voice and gloom and depression seemed to have a hold on him.

He was working out in the shed and when she had the kettle boiled, she called him in. She laid the table, sliced a rhubarb tart that she had made for him, and poured two mugs of strong tea. They sat in; he removed his cap, milked and suger'd his tea.

"Try a bit o' the tart, Johnny"

"Oh, thanks, I will."

"You're a bit depressed?"

"Ah, sure I suppose I am."

"D'ye play the music now a'tall?"

"Music! I wasn't down in that room since before she died."

"An' ye don't go out anywhere?"

"Damn the go! Campile for the shoppin' and te Mass, tha's all."

She topped up his mug, and her own.

"D'ye think ye might go out a bit after a while?"

"Sure where wud I be goin', Missis?"

"Ah sure, ye know … a concert … a dance … anywhere like that … where ye'd meet people."

"Ye'd want te be in good form for that."

"What d'ye think o' the tart?'

"'Tis raley lovely … I always like rhubarb."

"Ye might meet a nice woman."

His eyes widened with a look of embarrassment and disbelief that she would stray on to such a personal path.

"A woman! Sure I wouldn't know what te do wud a woman."

"Did ye never have a girl friend, Johnny?"

"Never had a steady wan."

"Have another bit o' tart."

He raised his hands.

"No no …full as a tick now."

"Why didn't ye?"

"Wha', Missis?"

"Never had a steady girl friend?"

"Ah, sure ye know yersef … how could I bring a girl in on top a me poor oul mother?"

"Wouldn't be very handy if ye had one now!"

He paused in thought, gazing into space. Molly could see that she had pricked his imagination.

"D'ye think so, Missis?"

"I do, Johnny."

Resuming eye contact, and with a rare smile lighting up his face, he exclaimed:

"Christ God! Ye could be right!"

*

It was mid-morning on Thursday, and it was such a beautiful July day that Molly felt an extra surge of energy and decided to use it productively. With the boys gone to school, the heifer, pigs and hens attended to, she turned her focus on the house. She made the beds, gave Granny her breakfast and set up a table of toys in the yard for Mina and Kenny to play in the sun.

She started on the windows and when she had them glistening, her basin of suds was black with the grime she had removed. She scrubbed the table, the shelves and the forms, and dusted the pictures and ornaments. The floor was next for a scrubbing. Granny sat in her chair by the fireside, oblivious to the hard work Molly was doing, and was even reluctant to move to the other side to allow the job to be completed. Molly was pleased with the new freshness, and would have loved to open all the windows, but she knew that wouldn't be allowed and didn't even suggest it.

Out in the yard, the sun was beaming down from a cloudless blue sky. In the lush grass of the little field, the heifer, pony and donkey, were lying off, sleeping contentedly in the heat. The big beech tree with its verdant summer cloak provided a lovely shade for the children as they played happily. Down the short grassy lane the hedgerows at each side were thick with all shades of summer foliage, and sweetly musical with joyous birdsong.

Molly was thrilled with the old rambler rose bush that had climbed the gable and spread over the car shed roof. It was in full bloom with hundreds of bright red roses adorning that corner of the little yard and sending sweet perfume to mix with the other mid-summer fragrances of plants and wild flowers. She wondered how old that rose bush was, and marvelled at the miracle of nature that sent such beauty every year without any prompting or reminding. She got a little idea. A big vase of roses would further adorn her sparkling kitchen. She climbed the wall and on to the car shed roof with an old shears. The perfume was overwhelming, the gable was a wall of red, she cut a huge bunch and made her way down. In the kitchen, she trimmed them on the table, placed them in a vase and set them into the window recess.

Granny wasn't impressed.

"That rose bush was planted by Tom's father fifty years ago, and that's the first time anyone cut them."

Molly didn't reply.

Mina and Kenny rushed in to the kitchen.

"Mammy! Mammy!" exclaimed Mina, "the postman is comin' up the lane."

Davy was a friendly postman. A small man about sixty, he had beads of sweat on his forehead, having removed his cap.

"God save ye, Missis … aint it a topper of a day."

"Oh, 'tis beautiful … it must be very hot on you though, carryin' that heavy bag."

'Oh, I'm used to it … it don't bother me atall."

He took out a bundle of letters, handed the top one to Molly.

"I have somethin' else here for ye too."

He searched his inside pocket, retrieved a folded note and gave it to her. She read the note:

Please collect a parcel at the post office in Campile.

"Oh, thanks, I'll collect that tomorrow when I'm gettin' the shoppin'"

"God be with ye now."

He walked down the short lane to his bike at the gate.

The letter was addressed to Granny and had an Italian stamp. From one of the nuns, Molly concluded and delivered it to her.

"That's from Agnes in Rome … I'd know her writing … open it for me."

It was a one page letter in perfect handwriting. Granny tried to read it but was having difficulty.

"Here, you better read it … my eyes are not the best."

Molly began:

Dear Mother,

I hope you are very well, as Mary and myself are, here in the Eternal City. You will be eighty on the first of August and every day we are offering our prayers and thanksgivings to Almighty God for blessing you with such a long life which we pray will continue for many more years.

Mother Superior has kindly granted us leave to return home to Ireland for a week to be with you on your great occasion. We will be staying at the convent in Wexford and will be able to travel out by motorcar.

We have written to Father Donovan and he has offered to celebrate a special mass for you and will visit you on the day with the Blessed Sacrament and a Blessing of Thanksgiving.

We hope that Tom, Peader and Tim will be present to make it a great occasion for you and for us all.

I will write again before we leave. Until then, may God and the Blessed Mother bless you and keep you.

Your loving daughter in Christ.

Sr. Agnes.

"They're coming … I knew they would … I'll be glad to see them."

"It'll be a great day," said Molly.

"I don't know where they're all going to fit," said Granny, with a questioning look at Molly.

"Oh, God, I don't know either … we'll have te see."

She already felt the burden of it all, even though it was still three weeks away. She got the feeling from reading that letter that she and the children might be in the way. Why was there no mention of them? The school would be closed and maybe Nellie or Nicky would take some of the children on holiday for that week. But she would prefer if they could be there for the celebration; they were her grandchildren and they should be part of it. She would have to think long and hard about it, an see what Tom thinks too.

The boys were up early; so early that they were able to enjoy seeing the early passenger train steam through the railway gates and puff its way along by the lower lane and up Knockea hill. It was an extra bonus for them on a special day. Not only was it Friday, the last day of the school week, but it was the end of the term and the start of the long summer holidays.

It was another beautiful morning and it promised to be a good day for their mother too. While she was doing the morning's housework, Paschal and Robbie caught the pony and yoked him to the trap. Timmy fed the pigs; Mina and Kenny let out the hens and chickens and collected the eggs. Tom had already milked the cow and had left for work.

With everything in order and the boys gone to school, Molly, Mina and Kenny climbed in to the trap and headed off to Campile. As the pony trotted evenly in the hot sun, he was soon feeling the pressure, and before he reached the village his neck and chest was covered in white foamy sweat.

'He's too hot, Mammy" said Kenny.

He'll be grand … he'll have an hour to rest an' dry off."

She tied him to the ring in the wall opposite the Co-Op store. It was a bit earlier than usual and she was glad that there were no queues at the counter like other Friday's. It didn't take long for her little written list to be turned into three bags of shopping, which they loaded into the trap. They then went across the yard to the outside store for flour, meal and paraffin oil, before visiting the chemist for Granny's medicine.

Molly always felt good when the week's shopping was done and when things went well on her Friday visit to Campile.

She felt even better as she steered the pony down the village towards the post office to collect the parcel that was too heavy for the postman to deliver.

It was the usual big square cardboard box, wrapped in strong brown paper with the white sticker on top declaring: '*Old Clothes*' and the name and address repeated on two sides. As she carried it out of the post office, she realised it was much heavier than usual and a hot surge of emotion filled her with love and gratitude for a sister as good and kind as Aggie.

After they had finished their lunch, tidied the house and had Granny organised, Molly and the two children went upstairs where the parcel was sitting on the double bed waiting to be opened. The scissors went to work and soon all was revealed. As each item of clothing emerged, the children gasped, their mother held them up and decided on the recipient, folded and placed them on the bed. The boys got pants, shirts and pullovers, and Mina got skirts, dresses and cardigans. Tom got two lovely shirts; one for working and one for Sunday. Molly wasn't left out. Two lovely frocks, a blouse and a long gabardine coat, all which fitted her perfectly.

One item emerged that surprised Molly. Hidden between the clothes was a real leather football. It had a bladder inside and lace tyings. All the air had been removed and only needed to be inflated and sealed. Molly knew that of all the things Aggie sent, the real leather football would be cherished most by the boys, would make their holidays more enjoyable, and she was delighted for them.

Timmy spotted his father coming through the railway gates and cycling along the lower lane. He had been on watch-out at the little gable window. His brothers were informed and a cheerful group ran down the lane to escort him home from work. Their big news story was the parcel of clothes from Aunt Aggie, and especially the real leather football.

"An' you got two lovely new shirts," exclaimed Robbie.

"Yeah, an' Mammy got lovely clothes too," said Timmy.

"Oh, begor, we'll be very swanky so."

Home in the yard, they showed him the football case.

"Will the bicycle pump blow it up?" asked Paschal.

"T'will, but we'll have te take a valve out of the bike wheel te connect it."

He unscrewed the valve, releasing all the air from the front wheel and fitted it tightly into the football bladder. The pump was connected and he held it on his knee while he pumped until it was full and hard. He then sealed the pipe, laced it up firmly and kicked it into the air to the delight of the boys.

"We'll have te put up proper goalposts now," said Paschal.

"But we have no poles," said Robbie.

'Maybe we might cut a couple," said their father.

He got the old bushman saw from the car shed. The ash trees that grew along the side of the field were fully clothed in their summer leaves. He searched for suitable branches and cut three of the straightest he could find. Having trimmed them and decided on a good spot for a football pitch, he made holes with the crowbar and set them firmly in the ground. When the crossbar was nailed on, they stood back and admired their creation.

"Now," said their father, "yis can play away an yis can think yis are in Croke Park."

"Thanks Daddy!" was repeated many times as he left them to their game and returned to the house.

After their early morning rise, the excitement of their last day in school before the holidays, and the intensity of the football game, the children were tired and sound asleep soon after climbing the little stairs. Granny went to bed early too, leaving Tom and Molly relaxing at the table enjoying tea and apple tart.

"'Tis only three weeks 'till yer mother's big day."

"I know ... t'won't be long comin' around."

"How will we manage atall, Tom? ... Where will we put 'em all?"

"Ah sure, they'll fit somewhere ... they'll be only here for wan day."

"I was thinkin' ... maybe Nellie or Nicky would take some of the children?"

Tom's eyes widened in surprise.

"We won't do that anyhow!"

"Why? Sure t'would make more room here ... an' the big lads would love to go."

"Ah no, ... this is goin' te be a big thing for us all, an' I'd like 'em te be here."

"Alright then. ... we'll have te manage someway ... but there won't be room te stir."

"Ah ... they'll be room enough." With a cute little smile and a twinkle in his eye he continued: "As the fella said: where one'll fit, two'll fit."

She reached over and with an anticipating smirk, took his hand in hers.

"C'mon then ... we'll see!"

They crossed the kitchen and quietly headed upstairs.

CHANGE OF PLANS

The Friday shopping list was twice its normal length. Molly had spent a long time compiling it the night before. She was looking forward to it, thinking it would be a labour of love, but the pleasure was gone out of it. She had expected Granny to stump up with enough money to cover the extra shopping expenses for her big day on Wednesday. But although she made a big deal of contributing, the three pounds she gave was only a fraction of the cost. Ten pounds would be nearer the mark.

Molly complained to Tom that it was not fair that their few pounds of savings should be spent on "wining an dining' all those people. It was Granny's big day and she should foot the bill.

"Ah I know, but sure she thinks ye wouldn't want much extra."

"Maybe so, Tom, but *you* should tell 'er ... I couldn't open me mouth."

"Ah, 'tis better say nothin'."

"Why, Tom? ... *She* have a lot more than we have, an nothin' te spend it on."

"I know. I know. But sure in a week's time t'will be all over ... better not have a row."

"Yer too soft with 'er, Tom, she's gettin' away too asy altogether."

"Ah sure."

When she arrived home from Campile, Molly had six bags of shopping instead of the usual three. She placed them on the table, hoping that Granny, seeing the big pile of extra expensive shopping, might feel guilty and revisit her purse. But it was not to be. She just glanced at them, turned away and returned to her semi-sleeping mode.

With the shopping stored away, and everyone full-bellied after lunch, Molly headed out to the yard. The cow house, pig house and hen house hadn't been mucked out for a while, and with the boy's help, she began the work. Tom would do them on his Saturday half-day, but she felt it wouldn't be fair on him. He would have worked hard enough all the week without having to work again at home.

It was a warm afternoon and they were sweating from the hard work. Granny appeared with her walking stick and shuffled her way out the yard and down the short grassy lane. She usually went as far as the gate where she would linger for a while in the sun, viewing and admiring the wide expanse of the bog.

After about half an hour, it occurred to Molly that Granny hadn't returned and she wondered had she passed by and into the house unnoticed. When she looked, she saw that the gate was half open and concluded that she had gone a bit further. After a while she began to get concerned and went down to the gate. She looked right, over towards Moran's, and left, down to the railway line. There was no sign of Granny in either direction. Thinking that she might be back inside, she hurriedly went back to the house; no sign of her there either. She went upstairs to the little gable window and took a sweeping look along the lower lane by the railway. She spotted the dark figure slowly moving back in the direction of the house. Relieved, she told the three boys to go down the lane to make sure Granny was alright, and to see if she wanted help to get home.

It took half an hour for them to return. Granny was exhausted and sweating. Molly gave her a drink and her medicine.

"Ye went a long way!"

She was out of breath and barely able to speak.

"It was such a nice day ... I went too far."

Molly put a pillow behind her head and she soon dozed off asleep. When she woke up, she said she felt cold and shivering. Molly took her to her room and helped her to bed.

Granny had been restless all night; sweating, coughing and trying to catch her breath. Tom and Molly didn't get much sleep either. When morning came, Molly suggested that he shouldn't go to work. It was Saturday and he would only miss half a day.

Granny hadn't touched the breakfast that Molly had given her on a tray. Her wheezing had become louder and squeaky.

'Would ye like anything else?"

No, was the reply, with a dismissive hand wave.

"Would ye like us to get the doctor for ye?"

With an even more emphatic hand wave, she dismissed the idea.

Molly knew she had made a mistake in asking. Whatever chance Tom would have had in convincing her to get the doctor, she was the one person that had no chance. Back in the kitchen, she was worried and uneasy. She made tea and called in Tom and the children.

"You go down, Tom, an' see what ye think."

He came up with a worried look on his face.

"She's no better ... she's worse, if anythin' ... will we get the doctor?"

"I said that to her an' she won't agree."

"She'll have to agree."

They both went down. Her wheezing had a whistling sound, her lips had turned blue, and her heart seemed to be racing. She had a frightened look in her eyes.

"We'll get the doctor for ye, Mother," said Tom.

She didn't reply.

Tom went over to Moran's. Johnny went immediately in the motorcar. Tom went back to help Molly prepare for the doctor.

It was mid-day when Doctor Maher drove into the yard in his big black motorcar. The gate at the end of the short lane had been left open for him and the children had been sent out to the field to play football.

Molly took him to Granny's bedroom. She left them and returned to the kitchen where Tom and herself waited anxiously.

They heard him emerge from the bedroom, met him halfway and took him to the kitchen.

'She's a very ill woman ... she can't stay here ... I'm removing her to hospital."

"Is she very bad, Doctor?" asked Tom.

"Well, as you know, she has had Chronic Bronchitis for a long time."

They both nodded their heads in agreement.

"But now she has developed a serious Exacerbation."

They waited wide-eyed for an explanation.

"In simple terms, it's a worsening of symptoms ... Dyspnea, Cough and sputum ... in other words, an infection has clogged up her lungs and affected her breathing."

"Is she in any danger, Doctor?" asked Molly.

"The danger is Pneumonia ... if that developed ..."

He pursed his lips and didn't finish the sentence. They got the message.

"When will she go, Doctor?" asked Molly.

"We'll have to send the ambulance for her ... this afternoon ... they'll bring her to the County Hospital in Wexford."

"Alright, Doctor, thanks very much," said Tom.

He was about to leave when he paused and turned towards Molly.

"This is a very small house ... how many children have you?"

Molly named them and gave the ages of each one.

"My God, that's a big family in such a small house!"

"It is," said Molly.

It was four o'clock, and the bright sunshine was beginning to fade. From the west, low, dark clouds were approaching and would soon slide under the sun, casting a dark shadow over the bog. Tom had been making preparations for the arrival of the ambulance. The pony's trap was moved out of the yard into the little haggard to make room for turning. The old wooden gate at the end of the short grassy lane was removed from its hangings and laid against the stone wall. The extra few inches would be of benefit to a wide vehicle.

The three older boys kept close to their father. They had many questions for him. The doctor, the ambulance and the hospital were all new things for them and they wanted to get a full understanding of it all. He tried to explain it as simple as he could, giving the impression that it wasn't really a crisis, and was something that most families had to deal with. Old people get sick, they go to hospital and get treatment, and then, with God's help, they come home well again.

Molly spent most of the time in the bedroom with Granny. She was much calmer and seemed to be resigned to being moved to hospital. The doctor's medication had eased her wheezing, but she was weaker and kept dozing into short periods of uneasy sleep.

The children were not brought to the bedroom. Molly discussed it with Tom, but they decided against it. Granny was too sick, she hadn't asked for them and maybe it would be better for her and for them.

Robbie was the first to spot the ambulance. It was easing its way slowly over the potholes of the lower lane by the railway. From the gable window, he shouted down to his father in the kitchen. Tom brought the news to the bedroom and the children headed for the football field. Their mother had told them to stay away from the yard and the house until the ambulance was gone. They didn't mind that because they could watch through little openings in the hedge, and without being seen, they had a full view of everything that happened in the yard.

The driver expertly manoeuvred the big white ambulance up the short lane, into the yard, turned and reversed back close to the kitchen door. He jumped out, opened the rear doors, and while he was organising things there, the nurse, a tall, middle-aged woman, dressed all in white, went with Molly to the bedroom.

The children were behind the hedge, each with a viewing point into the yard; careful not to cough or make a sound.

As she was too weak to stand up or walk, Granny was eased gently on to the stretcher and wrapped up comfortably for the journey that would take about an hour. Tom and Molly were offering to help, but the driver and nurse preferred to do it all themselves.

Steering the loaded stretcher out of the bedroom, through the little parlour, around the sharp corner of the hall, and out the narrow kitchen door was a tricky task, but they were well used to it, and Granny was soon placed in the ambulance, strapped in and ready for the road.

Before the doors were closed, Tom and Molly took her thin, bony hands in theirs, and said goodbye. Slowly it moved out of the yard, down the short lane and away, leaving a sad emptiness and an eerie silence. Molly embraced Tom when she saw a tear emerge and flow down his cheek.

The children returned. Words were hard to find. They all slowly moved inside, with anxious minds and heavy hearts.

DARK DAYS

Tom didn't go to work on Monday. On his way home from Sunday mass, he had cycled around by Jock Sullivan's to let him know. He got lots of sympathy, understanding, and good wishes for his mother's recovery.

"Take as many days as ye want, Tom, there's no big rush here at the moment."

Tom was grateful but said he would probably sort things out on Monday and be back to work on Tuesday.

"No problem, Tom, come back whenever yer ready."

Johnny Moran had offered to drive him to Wexford hospital and when they had finished their few jobs in the morning, they set off.

Molly had planned a busy day too. She would give Granny's bedroom a complete make-over. The bedclothes and curtains would be washed, the walls and floor would be scrubbed, and plenty fresh air would flow in through the open window and door. She would then head over the lane and do some extra housework for Johnny after he being so good to drive Tom to Wexford.

The first stop for Tom was the post office in Campile. Telegrams had to be sent to Peader and Tim. The postmistress, Mrs Dillon, helped him with the wording. They simply said: *Mother in Wexford hospital ... Not Good ... Tom.*

"When will they get 'em?" he asked anxiously.

"They'll have them in the next couple of hours ... as soon as they can be delivered."

"Oh, good, good, thanks very much," Tom was relieved to have that job done; it was like a weight off his shoulders.

Johnny drove on to the Duncannon New Line that led straight all the way to Wexford town. Their first call was to the St John Of God convent on the far side of the town; Tom had to get word to the nuns. He was welcomed by the Reverent Mother and escorted down a gleaming hallway to a luxurious sitting room. She sat him down at a big round polished table and told a young nun to bring tea.

He went through the whole sequence of events regarding his mother.

"Oh my God! And Sisters Agnes and Mary arriving from Rome tomorrow to celebrate her eightieth birthday on Wednesday."

"Yeah," said Tom, "they'll get a shock when they come."

"No ... I'll contact them today. I can phone from here to our house in Rome and I'll let them know."

"Oh, yeah, that would be great. Thanks very much."

"Yes ... it's better they know before they arrive ... and in the meantime our whole community will be praying for her."

"Thanks, Sister."

Tom was sorry for keeping Johnny so long waiting in the convent yard.

"God, Johnny, I couldn't help it ... 'tis hard te get out o' them nuns."

"Christ God, Tom, not a bother ... sure I was havin' a little snooze here."

They headed for the hospital.

At the reception desk, he was told to take a seat and wait. While he waited, he was surprised to see several visitors come in, report to the desk, and be directed up to the wards without any delay. Feeling a bit concerned and worried, he decided to report again to the desk. The young receptionist looked apologetic.

"Oh, I'm sorry, Sir ... Mrs Coonan is not allowed visitors at present ... but the doctor is coming down to speak with you."

Stricken with a surge of trepidation, he returned to his seat.

The doctor, young, tall and slim, with a long white coat, came briskly down the stairs and was referred to Tom by the receptionist.

"I'm sorry for keeping you waiting, Mr Coonan."

Tom stood up.

"Mrs Coonan is stable at present, but she is still critically ill ... she is on oxygen and strong medication, but as yet doesn't seem to be responding ... we are doing all we can for her."

Tom couldn't think of an intelligent question to ask.

"I can't see her?"

"She's very weak ... better to wait a little while."

"I'm after comin' a long way."

The doctor paused in thought.

"Alright then, Mr Coonan, come with me, and you can have a few minutes with her."

He followed the doctor up three flights of steps, along a bright corridor to a small end ward that had only a few beds. When he arrived at her bedside he was stunned to find her surrounded by screens and breathing through an oxygen mask. She seemed to know he was there but she appeared to be only half conscious. He took her hand and she responded with her eyes. He stayed only a few minutes and slowly moved away.

*

It was Wednesday, the first day of August 1950. It was well into the second half of 'The Holy Year.' More important for Tom, it was his mother's eightieth birthday.

Born in 1870, she had lived a good life, reared a good family, and despite ill-health, and her own pessimism, had reached the milestone of eighty years. He would love to see her live for many more years, but as Johnny Moran drove his motorcar around the centre circle of the hospital grounds, and the façade of the gloomy building appeared before him, he wasn't sure what to expect.

"I have no idea, Johnny, how long I'm goin' te be."

"Christ God Tom ... what the hell about it ...I'm in no hurry ... I'll go an' buy a paper an' I'll be readin' it in the motor car."

He climbed the steps, entered the wide reception area, and approached the desk. The young receptionist recognised him.

"Oh, Mr Coonan, I have been told to send you straight up to Ward 7 ... will you be able to find your way up?"

"Yes ... I think I know the way ... thanks."

Briskly, he climbed the three flights of steps and walked the long corridor. At the entrance to the ward he paused and gazed across to the far side. He could only see the high screens; the bed was completely surrounded. Gingerly, he tip-toed across the ward, careful not to disturb the other patients. As he got nearer, he could hear the course breathing and whispering behind the curtains. He entered. What filled his eyes rendered him speechless and overwhelmed him with emotion.

With her mouth open, struggling desperately to breathe, his mother appeared to be dying. His two sisters, Agnes and Mary, and his brothers, Peader and Tim, sat on chairs around the bed, tearful and whispering fervent prayers. They stood up. The nuns embraced him and his brothers shook his hand.

"How is she?" He was barely able to whisper the words.

"Very soon, she'll be in the arms of Jesus and Mary," said Agnes.

The others nodded their heads in agreement.

Nothing else was said but there was a sense of togetherness, that the circle was now complete and that they were all there to share a very sad, but precious moment.

Sister Agnes led the rosary and suggested they all say one mystery each. They didn't kneel but sat on the chairs with their gaze focussed on their dying mother. Voices were kept low and the murmuring prayer was interspersed with the rasping sound of laboured and erratic breathing. After the first mystery, Mary led the second and Peader the third. Sister Agnes announced: *The fourth Glorious Mystery: The Assumption of Our Blessed Lady into Heaven.*

Tom started the *'Our Father.'* He had only reached the third *'Hail Mary'* when the breathing suddenly stopped. The praying stopped too. They all moved closer, and in the eerie silence, stroked and kissed their dead mother.

"We will finish the rosary," said Agnes.

They moved the chairs back, and kneeling by the bed, the heartbroken group completed the last two mysteries. As they came near the end of *'The Hail Holy Queen'* the last little invocation had a special significance for the grieving family.

'May Thy Divine Assistance remain always with us, and may the Souls of the Faithful Departed, through the mercy of God, Rest in Peace. Amen.'

*

It was quiet and sombre around the breakfast table in the little kitchen. Since the news was brought home by their father the night before, the children had changed from their normal boisterous chatter, to an almost whispering mode, asking questions; sharing and discussing the mystique of it all.

Their mother was sparing and careful with her words too. She could sense Tom's anguish. In the privacy of the night and the togetherness of the pillow, he had shed many tears. She had cried with him, not from grief or mourning on her part, but in love and empathy for her nearest and dearest soul-mate, in his hours of suffering.

She too, had lost her mother and father, and knew the pain well. She tried to console him by dwelling on the gift of Granny reaching eighty years, and the blessing of having all her five children, by some miracle, around her bed, to bid farewell at her departure. But she knew that words of comfort wouldn't fill the emptiness that he felt. The little kitchen was full of that mysterious emptiness. The old armchair by the fireside, now empty and redundant. The cup, saucer and plate - more reminders of the vacancy - and the absence of her unique presence was an eerie sensation that only time would erase.

Tom's grief and anguish would be eased a little throughout the busy day ahead. The funeral arrangements, the grave digging, the Mass, and many other things had to be organised. As always, Johnny Moran came up trumps, putting himself, his motorcar, and his cheerful companionship at Tom's disposal.

Molly and the children watched as the the two men drove down the lane on their sombre mission that could take most of the day, and as they disappeared out of sight, returned to the gloom and loneliness of the little thatched house.

She had important work to do too. It was something she had been planning for over a week, but it had now taken a strange, new meaning. The meal of celebration for Granny's big birthday was postponed by two days, but would now be held after the funeral to-morrow. The only difference was that the guest of honour would not be there. But all the family would, including the nuns, Peader, Tim, Tom and themselves.

110

She saw it as a huge challenge, but one that she was determined to overcome. She would spend the day making the preparations and it would be as good as she could possibly make it. For Tom's sake, she would ensure that they would all be welcomed and entertained, and have no complaints from their return visit to their old homestead.

*

The congregation stood to attention as the twenty-four priests filed out from the sacristy for the High Mass and Office. Father Donovan, the chief celebrant, and his three co-celebrants, in their ornate black vestments, climbed the alter steps; the other twenty priests in their white surplices and black soutanes, took their positions in the front seats, surrounding the coffin.

The little church was filled with parishioners who had come to pay their respects and bid farewell to an elderly woman of the parish that they all knew of, but hadn't really known.

In the top seats were her daughters, Sister Agnes and Sister Mary, her sons, Tom, Peader and Tim, her daughter-in-law, Molly, and her grandchildren, Mina and Kenny. Her three grandsons, Paschal, Robbie and Timmy, were made alter boys for the ceremony, and though it was a new experience for them, their mother was proud of them in their white and red robes and the efficient way they performed.

Molly was impressed with the ceremony, the solemnity of it, and the intensity of spiritual fervour. Before the mass started the alter was incensed, and as the unique perfume wafted around the church, she could sense the respect and esteem that Granny enjoyed in the local church, especially among the clergy and the religious.

As the Requiem Mass began and the chorus of priests chanted the 'Kyrie Eleison' with gusto and passion, Molly knew that wherever Granny was, she would be enjoying it, content in the belief that her long life of prayer and austerity deserved it. Not many could afford a ceremony like that – each priest got a pound for his presence – but as Father Donovan had told Tom, Granny had saved up and had paid him for it, well in advance. No wonder the priest was so fulsome in his praise and admiration for her when he gave his eulogy. Molly was tempted to smile wryly when he said that *she was a saint and an example to all, with her life of prayer, compassion and love.*

She resisted the temptation, but kept her reservations deep in the crevices of her heart, knowing that her idea of compassion and love was somewhat different.

The old cemetery behind the church was now closed to new burials. For over two hundred years its old ivy-clad stone walls had enclosed the resting places of many generations of the faithful departed. When Granny's coffin was carried through the little arched entrance to the open grave across the way, the slow shuffling procession of mourners that followed, knew that she would soon be reunited with her husband, Mike, who had lain there waiting for her for over twenty years.

As the coffin was gently lowered and finally rested on the deep floor, each of her grandchildren stepped forward and dropped a red rose in, red roses from her beloved old rose bush, and as Molly held Tom's hand, a tear at last escaped, and trickled down her cheek.

*

Molly's apprehension intensified as she welcomed the Coonan family to their old homestead and ushered them into the little parlour. After the emotional stress of the funeral ceremonies for their mother, they seemed to be relieved to arrive and relax for a while in the old familiar surroundings that they all knew so well. This was the place of their birth, where they grew up, from where they went to school, and the scene of many of their childhood memories.

The tiny room had to be rearranged by Molly to ensure they fitted in comfortably. The polished mahogany table in the centre had its hinged leafs extended, a white, embroidered cloth draped it, and the old china delft and silver cutlery, gleamed in a dinner setting that had tested her skill and imagination.

The seating arrangements were planned too. Two chairs at each side and one at each end was all the table could take. Sister Agnes and Peader sat on one side, opposite Tim and Sister Mary. Tom took the chair on the far end, while the chair on the end nearest the kitchen was reserved for herself, but as she was serving, she didn't occupy it until later.

The children sat around the table in the kitchen for their meal, and were warned by their mother to keep their voices down and be of their best behaviour.

Although feeling a little tension, Molly was confident that her work and preparations over the past two days would make the occasion successful. She had worked in a big house in Waterford before she met Tom and knew what was required when cooking for visiting guests.

The four-course meal she had prepared yesterday, and was now serving, was important for her, and for Tom too. She hoped it would impress his brothers and sisters and help to restore to her some of the dignity and self-esteem that their mother had taken from her.

In a friendly, calm and relaxed atmosphere, they all seemed to savour the bowls of thick soup with home-baked brown bread and country butter, the boiled bacon with mashed potatoes and carrots in white sauce, the bowls of custard and jelly, and the cups of strong tea with jam scones. Molly was pleased to see their enjoyment of her efforts and she really appreciated the compliments that followed, which she knew were honest and sincere.

The conversation flowed freely, and all expressed pleasure that the little parlour they loved, had not been changed over the years. The old treasured pictures still adorned the walls. The wallpaper, embossed with flowery patterns, continued to give a warm feel to the room, and as ever, in its pride of place, the big framed photograph of their mother and father, taken on their wedding day, looked down, as it did for over fifty years, from above the mantelpiece.

They reminisced about their life growing up, the old nostalgic memories, the loss of their father when they were all still young, and heaped praise on their dead mother for her great resilience and strength in coping with the loneliness of all those years on her own. She was now gone, and they shared examples of the strange feeling of emptiness and loss at her passing. A transition, a moving on, an end of an era, a chapter ending, a closed book; she was gone and they all felt the pain. But one thing they all agreed: their parents were now reunited in heaven and, from now on, they would be an even more powerful influence in all of their lives.

When a lull came in the exchanges, a call for the children to join them was made; Molly brought them down from the kitchen. It took a while for their shyness to abate, but soon, with the help of Tim's light-hearted wisecracks, they became talkative and plenty of chatter ensued.

Sister Agnes beckoned Mina to her side.

"You're going to be a nun, like you aunts, when you grow up, aren't you?"

"I don't know."

"Why not? Wouldn't you like to be a nun, Mina?"

"I might"

"Don't mind her!" said Tim, "you're goin' to meet a nice fella, an' get married, an' have a hape a children, aren't ye, Mina"

Mina had no answer to that idea which gave them all a little laugh. Robbie was keen to get a word in.

"I'm goin' te be a train driver … an' be drivin' the big steam injins."

"An' I'm goin' te be a jockey!" said Timmy.

The uncle that he was named after, replied:

"Oh, good man, Timmy, we'll all make money then backin' ye in the races."

Paschal was quiet and reflective. Sister Mary took him to her side.

"You're going to be a priest, Paschal, aren't you?"

"I don't know," he replied with a shy smile.

"Oh, you will … and you'll have a big house and a big motorcar, and everyone will be saluting you, and calling you, Father."

"Begor," said Tom, "t'wouldn't be a bad job a'tall … plenty money in it anyway."

"An' what about this little chap," said Tim, lifting Kenny on to his knee, "what will you be when y'ill be big?"

"A farmer."

"Good man! Good man Kenny! A great life … sure I'm a farmer meself … now Tom … y'ill have te show this little man all about farmin' … the best job of 'em all."

Molly was catching up with her own meal at the end of the table and enjoying the light-hearted banter. Peader intervened in a little more serious tone.

"No matter what ye want to be, the main thing is to keep at school and get secondary education."

Sister Agnes, who, like Peader, had many of Granny's ways and ideas, agreed with him.

"Oh yes, ye must keep going to school and then ye will get good careers."

"Ah," said Tim, "I know fellas that never went a day te school in their lives an' they made fortunes."

"That may be so," said Peader sternly, "but that would be the exception."

"Don't mind that Uncle Tim," said Sister Mary, "that fella never stops joking ... keep learning and going to school, and ye won't regret it."

Tim laughed and the children laughed with him.

Before leaving, the nuns gave the children a rosary beads each; they gave Tom an ornate leather wallet, and to Molly they gave a pearl rosary beads, blessed by the Pope. Tim gave a shilling to each of the children, and Peader gave Molly a pound for herself, and a pound to buy something for the children.

They all walked down the short grassy lane to the hackney car that had returned to take them home. Tom, Molly and the children went with them. It was a nostalgic stroll and nothing around the old homestead went unnoticed. When expressing their appreciation for the lovely meal and the pleasant visit, they each said that they would come again soon and perhaps stay a little longer. Molly, in her heart, wondered about that, and if anyone would be there to receive them.

As the doors of the big motor car slammed closed and the waving began, a strange feeling of closure gripped Molly. It had been a traumatic few days for them all, especially for Tom. The sequence of events and the frenzy of activities helped to concentrate minds, but now it was all over, and in the calm aftermath, a new beginning awaited.

The receding vehicle finally disappeared out of sight. The family, huddled in a little group, relaxed and waited for someone to say something. But words weren't easily found. Tom broke the silence.

"That's it then."

Molly took his hand.

The bog was darkening, changing its shades of green to reflect the fading light from the setting sun. It was also reflecting the darkness that cast a deep shadow over the family as they strolled back to the little thatched house.

Molly knew in her heart that it would pass. To-morrow would be a new day. Life would go on, and with hope, togetherness and love, they would all go with it.

EPILOGUE

Molly stood with her arms folded in the dazzling brightness of her new kitchen. The two big windows soaked in the mid-day autumn sun, and gave her a panoramic view of the lush South Wexford landscape.

It was early October, and although it would soon be winter, she was now ready, willing and able to contend with whatever the future held in store.

In the solitude of her new, beautiful surroundings, and the peaceful contentment of her heart, she reflected on how the past year had transformed her life, and the lives of her family. Even now, she found it hard to comprehend the huge crossing they had made, from the gloom and isolation of their existence in a little thatched homestead on the edge of a bog, to their new life in this beautiful cottage just outside the bustling village of Campile.

Although it was only a month since they moved in, she was thrilled with the things that had happened since. All the five children were now attending Ballyhack school, a new modern building, run by the Sisters from the St. Louis convent, and only a short distance from their home. Tom had started his new job as a lorry driver in the Shelburne Co-Op, a challenge that has uplifted his spirit and given him a new sense of status and esteem.

Looking across the little field that came with the cottage, and sharing the peace and contentment of the cow and pony, resting in the sun, she silently noted in her mind the sequence of events that led them from that dark Limbo to this Heavenly bliss.

It was her unflinching determination to succeed, Doctor Maher's efforts in her quest for a new house, and Tom's loving co-operation, in eventually conceding to her endless cajoling, to leave his old homestead for this new life. He resisted bravely for a while, but could not hold out against the weight of his children's pleading, and her intensified love and affection.

But, as she now realised, everything had a price tag. That intense love may have won over her husband's mind, but it also did something else. She looked forward to his arrival home from work, sitting him down, and telling him the news, that their new home would soon have an extra little member of the family.

It wasn't planned by her or by Tom. Perhaps it was the Mother of God, in return for all the favours granted, that had set her this new task. If that was so, and she now believed it was, she was willing and happy to oblige.

End.

OTHER BOOKS
BY PADDY CUMMINS

Dark Secrets

Green Lodge

Dream Valley

The Crying Sea

The Long Road

It's a Long Way to Malta

In Love with Malta

Malta & Gozo

At Home in Ireland

Doctor Google

The Magic of Copper

Lyrical Ireland

Dream Valley
Paddy Cummins

Jenny seemed to have everything.

Fearless and talented in the saddle. Brilliantly distinguished in the boardroom. Beautiful and sensational in the bedroom. She was still unfulfilled, searching. Why?

Her handsome, older, doting husband, Dr. Ken McKevitt, knew the answer. Devastated by his failure, consumed with intense possessive love, he tried desperately to hold on to her.

Gary Wren, a stunning young racehorse trainer had just 'arrived' in the beautiful Green Valley of South Kilkenny.

Fate played its devastating hand in locking all three together in an intriguing and turbulent saga, winning Jenny her greatest prize; her husband, his peace of mind.

The reward was great, but the cost was even greater.

Green Lodge
Paddy Cummins

The equine bloodlines developed by Janet Johnson at Green Lodge Stud Farm are the secret of her brilliant success.

Her human bloodlines are a secret too, but they would lead her to turmoil, strife and dismal failure. The dream of nineteen-year-old, penniless, stable lad, Ricky Baker, to one day, own a stud farm, takes an unexpected turn with the chance discovery that his wealthy Farmer/Politician boss, is not the Sam MacArdy he thought he was.

It is the first step on a journey that would lead him to Gillian, and change their lives forever.

So begins two years of adventure, excitement, ecstasy, passion, pain and torment.

His dream and Gillian's true love are the powerful strengths that bring them through.

The Crying Sea
Paddy Cummins

A Maltese fishing boat explodes in a raging inferno and sinks to the depths of the Mediterranean.

So begins six days and nights of unspeakable anguish for the crew; shock, horror and grief for the whole island of Malta.

Inspired by a true sea disaster …

A harrowing story of intense human drama.

"A superb read … A story that will remain with you forever."
Damien Tiernan. RTE. Irish Television.
Author of:
'Souls Of The Sea'
Now a Major Film 'SIMSHAR'

It's a Long Way to Malta
Paddy Cummins

An Irishman's 'Gem in the Med'

"Paddy Cummins has created a gripping and emotional book that captivates at every turn of the page. Endlessly fascinating, tensely absorbing, with humorous anecdotes, this is classic travel writing – a brilliant read".
Michael K Hayes. Renowned Travel Writer. BBC Radio Presenter.

Dark Secrets
Paddy Cummins

This is the true story of incredible events in the life of a little farm family in Ireland over the last fifty years.
Lovingly Warm and Tender
It will intrigue, delight and fascinate.

Lyrical Ireland
Paddy Cummins

Fruit for the Soul

From the tree of Life

A collection of Paddy's Poems

First published in 2018

At Home In Ireland
Paddy Cummins

**A charming collection of
Short Stories and Poems**

Stories Rich and Real

Poems Sweet and Tender

A Flavour of Ireland

The Long Road
My Journey
Paddy Cummins

An autobiography, a memoir, a journey, a life.

Review. By Sheila

"I like the way Paddy has the ability to write about himself with true honesty & grit, without losing his natural warmth & good-natured spirit.

I consider it a real privilege to be included in surveying his personal path through life, his trials & tribulations and all expressed with clever wit and Irish blarney".

ABOUT THE AUTHOR

Paddy Cummins is the author of seventeen books. His four novels are best sellers on Amazon. His two travel books are multiple number ones and his epic sea book is now the story of a major film. He lives in Ireland during the summer months and in Malta during winter.

Follow Paddy at: www.irelandtoday.net

Printed in Great Britain
by Amazon

43703154R00080